Generative AI Demystified

Transforming Ideas into Action: Unlock the Power of AI

Nishant Srivastava
Dr. Akhilesh Kumar Sharma

ARCCHIE
www.arcchieonline.com

Generative AI Demystified

Transforming Ideas into Action: Unlock the Power of AI

Editor: Shambhu
Production Manager: Gaurav Mutreja
Cover design by Freepik and Vecteezy
Formatting & Indexing: Rahul

First Edition: Apr-2025
Reference: 2409134
Published by Arcchie Publications

ISBN-13 (paperback): 978-81-986981-7-9
ISBN-13 (eBook): 978-81-979768-9-6

www.arcchieonline.com

DEDICATED TO

To my wife Sukriti and my two sons Vedant and Rudra —your love, patience, and unwavering belief in me have been my most significant source of strength. This journey would not have been possible without your endless support and encouragement.

- Nishant Srivastava

To the almighty God, my Parents, my wife, Manisha, and my brothers, their unconditional support and patience have been my greatest source of strength. Their encouragement gave me the strength to dedicate myself to fulfilling and achieving my goals.

- Dr. Akhilesh Kumar Sharma

ACKNOWLEDGMENTS

Writing this book has been an incredible journey—one that extends far beyond the act of structuring words on a page. It has been a shared endeavor enriched by the wisdom, encouragement, and unwavering support of many individuals who have shaped my understanding of Generative AI and fueled my passion for its transformative potential.
First and foremost, my deepest gratitude goes to my family. To my wife and my two sons—your patience, understanding, and constant encouragement have been my most significant source of strength. The late nights, endless research, and deep-dive discussions would not have been possible without your support. I would like to express my gratitude to my mentors and colleagues at Microsoft, whose insights, feedback, and technical expertise have played a pivotal role in shaping this work. The collaborative spirit and intellectual rigor that define our discussions have been instrumental in refining my perspectives on AI's evolving landscape. To the broader AI and research community, thank you for your invaluable contributions, papers, and discussions, which have continuously pushed the frontiers of knowledge. Your work has laid the foundation for this book. I am also immensely grateful to the individuals who took the time to share their experiences, case studies, and real-world applications of Generative AI. Your insights have enriched the content and reinforced the practical impact of these technologies across industries. I want to express my heartfelt thanks to my editorial team and publishing partners, whose meticulous attention to detail and unwavering commitment helped bring this book to life. Your dedication has transformed my vision into a polished and accessible guide. Finally, to you—the reader—whether you are a researcher, a technologist, or an enthusiast exploring the potential of Generative AI, this book is for you. I hope it serves as a guide, a source of inspiration, and a catalyst for deeper exploration. This book is a testament to the power of collaboration, curiosity, and shared knowledge. Generative AI is reshaping the world, and I am honored to contribute to this ever-evolving conversation.

Thank you all for being part of this journey.

- *Nishant Srivastava*

ACKNOWLEDGMENTS

Having an idea to write this book was as impressive as it seems. I passionately started writing the article, hoping this would help potential researchers and students learn and increase their skills in the latest generative AI-related solutions. I sincerely convey my gratitude to all the authors, researchers, and contributors who wrote this excellent book, which is a testament to all the efforts we have put in. The path was not very simple and was full of challenges, such as exploring, reading, and writing more. I am very happy and convey my deepest gratitude to my entire family, who greatly supported me in this journey of writing this book. They encouraged me in every facet of life and during the writing phase. I also mention all the mentors and colleagues at Manipal University Jaipur who directly and indirectly encouraged me and played a pivotal role in writing this wonderful book. The time we spent together discussing various great ideas related to Generative AI was great fun and instrumental to the success of this book. I also sincerely acknowledge the support provided by the leadership of Manipal University Jaipur, who gave me the opportunity and time to put my effort into releasing this wonderful book. I also express my sincere thanks to the support provided by the publishing team, the technical editorial committee, and the team for the success of this book. They constantly motivated and supported me while developing the content and writing the book. This book will provide the best possible knowledge about generative AI and related technologies. We hope that the learners will be able to implement the ideas and build real-time applications. Also, we hope that this insightful learning material will help create some socio-economic welfare applications and impact society at large.

Thank you all for being part of this journey.

- Dr. Akhilesh Kumar Sharma

ABOUT THE AUTHORS

With over two decades of expertise as a seasoned solution architect, **Nishant Srivastava** is currently working with Microsoft as an Architect within ISD's Global Engineering and Architecture group. His journey has been marked by a relentless pursuit of innovation, consistently delivering complex digital transformation projects for global clients. At the core of Nishant's success is his strategic vision and leadership. He has a unique ability to see the big picture while diving deep into the technical details. This combination of strategic thinking and technical expertise enables him to craft solutions that are not only innovative but also practical and aligned with business objectives. In his current role as Lead Architect for Gen AI-based Solution Accelerator, a cutting-edge generative AI solution revolutionizes business functions such as Procurement, HR, Finance, and Legal. He envisioned the concept, crafting it into a prototype, which he then nurtured into a comprehensive enterprise solution offering. His ability to forge strategic partnerships with the sales team has driven multiple customers' successful adoption of the accelerator, turning it into a multi-million-dollar services business. This success underscores his ability to identify market needs, innovate, and deliver solutions that meet and exceed expectations. Nishant's contributions have not gone unnoticed. Over the years, he has received numerous accolades that recognize his excellence in both technical and leadership capacities. Among these are the Microsoft CFO Award FY25, the EAG Vision Award FY24, the Rise Award for FY24 H1, the SPARK Award for Q3-FY21, and multiple Better Together Awards for various quarters spanning FY20 and FY21. In 2018, he was inducted into the prestigious Microsoft Circle of Excellence Gold Club, an honor reserved for the top-performing employees who demonstrate outstanding contributions to the company's success. He is a Microsoft Certified Azure Solutions Architect Expert, a Microsoft Certified Azure AI Engineer Associate, and a Microsoft Certified Azure Data Engineer Associate. Beyond technical certifications, Nishant is also a Prosci® Certified Change Practitioner and a Professional Scrum Product Owner™ I (PSPO I), highlighting his holistic approach to solution architecture and project management. His recognition as a Design Thinking Champ Gold further underscores his commitment to innovative problem-solving, ensuring that the solutions he architects, are technically sound, user-centric, and aligned with business goals. Beyond his professional achievements, Nishant is also an Industry External Member of the Board of Studies at Manipal University, Jaipur. In this role, he advises the institution on industry trends, helping to bridge the gap between academia and the rapidly evolving professional landscape. His insights have been instrumental in revamping the B. Tech\M. Tech syllabus for the Data Science stream, ensuring that it remains aligned with the latest industry demands and technological advancements.

ABOUT THE AUTHORS

Akhilesh Kumar Sharma is a distinguished Senior Member of both IEEE and ACM and boasts an impressive academic background with B.E., M.E., and Ph.D. degrees in Computer Science and Engineering (CSE). Currently serving as a Professor and Head of the Department (DSE) at Manipal University Jaipur (MUJ), India. His expertise extends globally, evidenced by his involvement in writing technical books and articles, chairing sessions, and delivering expert keynotes at prestigious institutions such as IITs and NITs in India and international venues in Vietnam, Thailand, Malaysia, Australia, and Singapore. His contributions are not limited to academia. He holds an impressive publication record with over 80 articles in esteemed journals and conferences of national and international repute, along with authored books and book chapters. Furthermore, his innovative research holds Ten patents and Six copyrights. His professional affiliations include Senior Memberships in ACM, IEEE, CSI, IUCEE, and the MIR Laboratory, USA, and membership in the Institution of Engineers of India. He has received numerous accolades for his contributions to the field. He serves as Secretary of the ACM Professional Chapter Jaipur, further demonstrating his dedication to advancing the profession connects. He is also working with the ACM India council and working towards Academia – Industry connects and strengthening the vision for the university and the country to realize the potential and impact to the society by providing the most outstanding innovative solutions and to inculcate the habit of studying hard in the young brilliant minds.

ABOUT THE TECHNICAL REVIEWER

Dr. Gaurav Aroraa is a distinguished Microsoft MVP award recipient and an influential  Mentor of Change with AIM NITI Aayog, Government of India. He is a business coach with Business Blaster, Government of NCT Delhi, and he contributes significantly to the startup ecosystem. Dr. Aroraa is a lifetime Computer Society of India (CSI) member. He holds certifications as a Scrum Trainer and Coach, ITIL-F, PRINCE-F, and PRINCE-P, showcasing his expertise in project management and IT service management. Dr. Aroraa is an accomplished open-source developer and an active contributor to the Microsoft TechNet community. With a rich background in technology, he has authored books across diverse fields, addressing both emerging and established technologies. His recent achievements include being recognized as a world record holder for his contributions to books in exceptional and cutting-edge technologies. Dr. Aroraa inspires professionals, educators, and students through knowledge-sharing initiatives and mentorship.

PREFACE

Generative AI Demystified: Transforming Ideas into Action is your comprehensive guide to transforming the power of Generative AI from the realm of theory into practical, impactful business solutions. This book is crafted to serve both technical experts eager to stay at the forefront of Generative AI advancements and curious newcomers looking to explore this transformative technology. With its hands-on approach, this guide demystifies the complexities of Generative AI, providing the tools and insights necessary to thrive in today's rapidly evolving landscape. Starting with the basics, the book lays out the evolution of Generative AI, breaking down its core principles and how it stands apart from traditional AI models. Readers will grasp how this technology is reshaping industries across the globe. You will move from understanding foundational concepts to the intricacies of Large Language Models (LLM) and Small Language Models (SLM), with a detailed exploration of when to deploy each based on real-world scenarios and business needs.

The heart of Generative AI lies in the efficient retrieval of information, which is where Vector Databases come into play. This book not only explains their importance but also shows you how to integrate them into AI solutions for maximum performance. The practical chapters on Retrieval-Augmented Generation (RAG), covering both Vector RAG and Graph RAG, provide you with a roadmap to enhance AI outputs by incorporating external data sources. They deliver insights and real-world examples to help you navigate this exciting technology. RAG versus Fine-Tuning? This book offers comparative analysis, clearly understanding when to use each approach, depending on your business context, performance goals, and cost considerations. Prompt Engineering, a crucial yet often overlooked aspect of AI, is thoroughly examined with tips and best practices that will allow you to extract the most accurate and relevant responses from your models.

However, it is not all about technology. In a world increasingly powered by AI, ethical considerations are paramount. The final chapter on Responsible AI delves into the principles of building AI systems that are not only effective but ethical and legally sound. From privacy concerns to bias mitigation, this chapter ensures that your AI innovations are aligned with responsible deployment and governance.

Whether you are interested in streamlining Procurement, optimizing HR functions, improving Legal processes, or transforming your Finance operations, this book offers real-world applications of Azure OpenAI for these horizontal business functions. Additionally, it addresses the unique challenges and opportunities of various industry verticals, such as Manufacturing, Automobile/Mobility, and Finance, showcasing how Generative AI can revolutionize them.

Throughout the book, you will find practical insights and actionable guidance that will enable you to turn ideas into transformative actions. With an emphasis on real-world business applications, Generative AI Demystified equips you with the knowledge and strategies to lead in a Generative AI-driven future.

Let's embark on this journey of learning together.

What's Inside This Book

Chapter 1: Basics of Generative AI introduces the foundational concepts of Generative AI, including its evolution, core principles, and how it differs from traditional AI models.

Chapter 2: Navigating Language Models Choosing the Right Model for the Right Task: Explore the difference between large language models (LLM) and Small Language Models (SLM) and their specific applications.

Chapter 3: Introduction to Vector Databases dives into the role of vector databases in enabling efficient information retrieval for AI models.

Chapter 4: Retrieval-Augmented Generation (RAG) talks about RAG to enhance AI-generated output by incorporating relevant data from external sources, focusing on Vector RAG and Graph RAG.

Chapter 5: RAG vs Fine-Tuning A comparative analysis of using RAG versus fine-tuning models to enhance AI performance.

Chapter 6: Introduction to Prompt Engineering Master crafting effective prompts for Generative AI to produce desired results.

Chapter 7: Frameworks to work with Azure OpenAI explores the frameworks for building AI solutions with Azure OpenAI, explicitly focusing on Lang Chain and Semantic Kernel. It provides insights into choosing the proper framework based on your project needs and objectives.

Chapter 8: Multi-Agent Framework and Design Principles explores the concept of multi-agent systems, and the design principles involved in building AI systems with multiple agents.

Chapter 9: Applying Azure OpenAI Solutions for Horizontal Functions covers real-world applications of Azure OpenAI across horizontal business functions like Procurement, HR, Legal, and Finance.

Chapter 10: Leveraging Azure OpenAI for Industry Verticals discovers how Azure OpenAI can be leveraged to meet the unique needs of specific industries like Manufacturing, Mobility, and Finance.

Chapter 11: Responsible AI focuses on AI's ethical, legal, and social implications, particularly its principles.

For Whom This Book Is Intended

This book is written with the beginner in mind:

- Business leaders looking to leverage AI for competitive advantage
- Technology professionals and architects seeking to implement Azure OpenAI solutions
- AI enthusiasts wanting to deepen their knowledge of practical AI applications
- Procurement, HR, Legal, and Finance professionals exploring Gen AI-driven transformation
- Industry specialists in Manufacturing, Automobile, and Banking sectors.

Errata

At **ARCCHIE Publications**, we are committed to delivering the highest-quality content in all our publications. We follow best practices to ensure the accuracy of our content to provide our readers with indulgent reading experience. We believe and understand that our readers are our best judges, and we always use their input and feedback from time to time to improve human errors, if any, that may occur during the publishing processes involved. We invite you to participate in our errata submission process to ensure our books remain accurate and up to date. Please help us reach out to readers who might have difficulties due to unforeseen errors. Please write to us at ***errata@arcchieonline.com***.

When submitting errata, please include the following information:
Book Title
Reference#
Author(s)
Page Number
Description of the Error
Suggested Correction (if applicable)

The **ARCCHIE Publications** Family highly appreciates your support, suggestions, and feedback.

Sharing Your Perspective and Providing Feedback

Your perspective is invaluable to us, as it helps us enhance our content and gather your feedback. We warmly welcome all forms of feedback. Please feel free to send us an email at **feedback@arcchieonline.com**, mentioning the book title in the subject line of your message.

Book Review Invitation

We kindly invite you to share your thoughts. After you've read and engaged with this book, consider leaving a review on the platform where you acquired it. Your impartial feedback can greatly assist potential readers in making informed decisions. Your reviews provide valuable insights for us at **Arcchie**, helping us better understand your perspectives on our products, and they offer authors the chance to appreciate your feedback on their work.

Piracy

Should you encounter unauthorized reproductions of our publications in any digital format on the internet, we kindly request your assistance in pinpointing their locations or website sources. Please reach out to us at **copyright@arcchieonline.com** and include a link to the infringing material.

If you possess expertise in a particular subject and wish to participate in the creation or contribution to a book, please visit ***authors.arcchieonline.com***. We welcome you and assist you to start your authorship journey with **ARCCHIE PUBLICATIONS**.

TABLE OF CONTENTS

1

Basics of Generative AI

In the brisk, digital dawn of November 2022, the world experienced a transformative shift in the landscape of artificial intelligence with the launch of ChatGPT. This revolutionary model, developed by OpenAI, did more than respond to questions. It engaged in conversations that felt strikingly human. For the first time, a machine could effortlessly weave words together to craft a compelling response; that is the kind of fluidity ChatGPT brought to the table. It was not just churning out robotic replies; it was creating nuance and depth text, leaving many to wonder if they were indeed chatting with a machine or a fellow human being.

This shift was more than a technological upgrade—it was a transformation that reshaped our understanding of what AI could be. I remember discussing a complex project with a colleague who was frustrated by the tedious task of user story creation. We decided to give ChatGPT a try when drafting user stories. Surprisingly, it generated detailed and well-structured stories with acceptance criteria and relevant scenarios. It felt more like collaborating with an expert who understood our project goals and methodologies. As the excitement of ChatGPT's debut rippled through the tech community, it became clear: we were stepping into a new age where machines could collaborate with us in ways we had never imagined. The potential applications seemed endless, and the collaboration between human ingenuity and machine intelligence opened up new horizons for innovation and problem-solving.

To grasp the significance of this moment, we need to peel back the layers of generative AI—its origins, the principles behind it, and the ambitions fuelling its growth..

We will cover the following topics:

- Evolution of Generative AI
- Understand the fundamentals of Generative AI and its potential for business transformation.

Evolution of Generative AI

Generative AI originated in 1966 with the development of ELIZA, the first chatbot created by MIT professor Joseph Weizenbaum. Designed to simulate a psychotherapist, ELIZA enabled users to input messages and generate responses through a pattern-matching approach. One of ELIZA's most famous scripts, "DOCTOR," rephrased user input as questions, mimicking human-like conversations. Although primitive by today's standards, ELIZA was one of the first systems to challenge the boundaries of human-computer interaction.

To better understand this milestone, it is important to consider the Turing Test, proposed by British mathematician Alan Turing in 1950. This test evaluates a machine's ability to demonstrate behavior indistinguishable from human interaction. Although ELIZA managed to pass the Turing Test for specific users, it only touched the surface of what conversational AI can achieve.

By 1972, the development of the first intelligent humanoid robot, WABOT-1, set the stage for advances in AI and robotics. However, despite these early breakthroughs, AI research faced significant setbacks during the First AI Winter (1975–1980) and Second AI Winter (1987–1993), where optimism dwindled due to technical limitations, unmet expectations, and cuts in research funding.

The Two AI Winters: Challenges and Lessons

The evolution of artificial intelligence (AI) has been characterized by remarkable advancements and notable challenges, often referred to as the AI Winters. Rather than merely being phases of stagnation, these times offered valuable insights that have significantly contributed to the progress we see in AI today.

The First AI Winter (1975–1980): A Cold Reality Check

The early excitement around AI was palpable, with scientists and visionaries predicting the dawn of machines with human-level intelligence. However, the First AI Winter arrived between 1975 and 1980, bringing a chilling dose of reality. Researchers faced significant computational limitations; the computers of the time could not process the vast amounts of data required. Additionally, insufficient data made it challenging to train AI models effectively.

An important milestone highlighting the difficulties of this period was the publication of the Lighthill Report in 1973. Commissioned by the British government and written by Sir James Lighthill, the report critically evaluated AI's advancements and prospects. Lighthill contended that AI had not fulfilled its expectations, especially regarding natural language processing and robotics. This pointed critique resulted in a significant decrease in funding for AI research in the UK, prompting similar responses in other countries.

Interestingly, during this same period, the rise of microcomputers was transforming the tech landscape. However, despite the increased availability of computing power, AI researchers could not leverage these advancements effectively due to the inherent limitations of the algorithms and data available at the time.

The Second AI Winter (1987-1993): Thawing the Ice

The Second AI Winter, which lasted from 1987 to 1993, emerged due to AI's commercial setbacks and disappointing performance in real-world applications. Despite the considerable excitement surrounding AI at that time, many systems fell short of expectations, resulting in substantial reductions in research funding. A notable cause of this decline was the downfall of the Lisp Machine market.

Lisp Machines were specialized computers tailored for executing Lisp, a programming language widely utilized in AI research. Companies such as Symbolics and LISP Machines Inc. emerged as pioneers in this market, initially generating considerable excitement for their products. However, the high costs associated with these machines hindered their widespread adoption. As general-purpose computers grew more powerful and affordable, the niche market for Lisp Machines diminished, ultimately resulting in the financial decline of these companies and fueling a broader sense of disillusionment with AI.

Despite these setbacks, the AI community used this period for crucial reflection and recalibration. Researchers began to rethink and refine AI methodologies, focusing on more achievable goals and laying the foundational work for the machine learning and data-driven approaches that dominate the field today.

Resurgence and Milestones in AI

Despite these challenges, significant advances emerged in the 1980s and 1990s. Michael Toy and Glenn Wichman pioneered procedural content generation in the game Rogue. Judea Pearl's work on Bayesian networks revolutionized probabilistic reasoning, while Michael Irwin Jordan advanced recurrent neural networks (RNNs).

In 1989, Yann LeCun and colleagues introduced convolutional neural networks (CNNs), transforming the field of image recognition. Fei-Fei Li's ImageNet database, launched in 2006, provided a vast training dataset for visual object recognition.
By the early 2010s, significant advancements in AI had taken shape: IBM's Deep Blue triumphed over the world chess champion in 1997, while the Roomba emerged as a popular AI household device in 2002. In 2013, Google's word2vec revolutionized machine understanding of semantics.
In 2014, researchers from the University of Montreal introduced a groundbreaking concept called Generative Adversarial Networks (GANs). Think of GANs as a creative duel between two models: one tries to create something (the generator), while the other tries to judge if it is accurate or fake (the discriminator). It is like an art student trying to paint a masterpiece good enough to fool an art critic, and in doing so, both improve their skills. This technique brought us marvels like StyleGAN, which can generate incredibly realistic images.

One year later, smart folks at Stanford and UC Berkeley developed Diffusion Models. These models work like sculptors, starting with a rough noise block and gradually refining it to produce something beautiful and coherent. The magic behind the stunning images from systems like Stable Diffusion lies here.

Fast forward to 2017, and researchers at Google unveiled the Transformer architecture, revolutionizing how we handle text. Imagine reading a book where every word is given special attention, understanding its relationship with every other word. That is what transformers do, enabling technologies like ChatGPT to craft human-like conversations.

Generative AI - Introduction

Generative AI is artificial intelligence capable of producing new content—such as text, images, music, or code—by recognizing patterns in existing data. In contrast to traditional AI, which primarily concentrates on data analysis and classification, generative AI advances this concept by creating new outputs that emulate human creativity.
At its core, Generative AI relies on complex algorithms, most of which are powered by neural networks, to learn patterns in data and produce new content based on that understanding. These models are trained on vast datasets to extract the underlying structure and context, enabling them to generate fresh outputs that are contextually relevant. This could range from writing human-like articles to generating lifelike images, audio, or code. What makes generative AI particularly powerful is its ability to create new data that is not explicitly part of its training—enabling applications across multiple domains like content creation, design, software development, and more.

We investigate the key architectures that power generate AI to understand this.

The Backbone Models of Generative AI

Diffusion Models

Diffusion models work by starting with random noise and gradually removing it to produce high-quality, realistic outputs. Think of it like photo restoration, where you start with a grainy, unclear image and progressively sharpen it to reveal the original clarity.

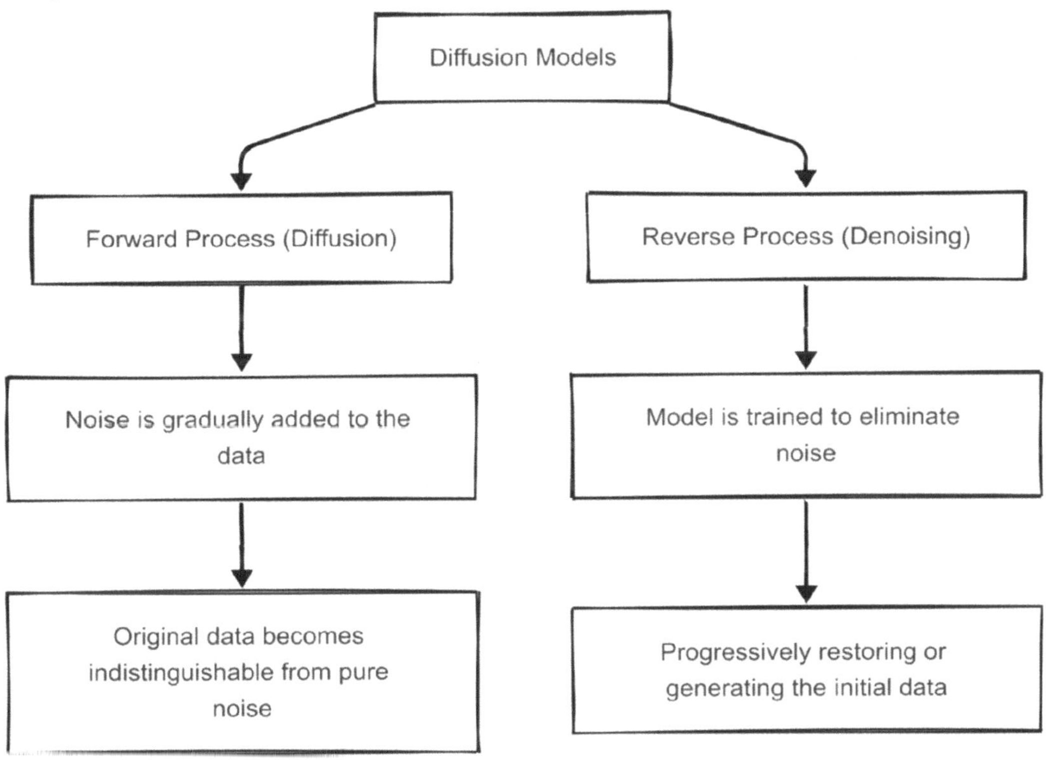

Fig 1.1 two-stage process of Diffusion Models

This image illustrates the working of diffusion models in two stages. The Forward Process (Diffusion) involves gradually adding noise to the data until it becomes indistinguishable from pure noise. The Reverse Process (Denoising) trains the model to eliminate the noise progressively, restoring or generating the initial data.

The **diffusion process** can be described in two stages:

- **Forward Process (Diffusion)**: This is where noise is gradually added to the data in small, controlled increments until the original data becomes indistinguishable from pure noise.

- **Reverse Process (Denoising)**: At this stage, the model is trained to systematically eliminate noise, progressively restoring or generating the Initial data.

Example 1: Image Generation

Let us consider an example where we want to generate high-resolution images from noise. The model starts by taking an image of a cat, for instance, and then iteratively adds random noise until the image looks like random static (essentially, no meaningful image remains). This noisy version of the image is then fed into a neural network during training. The **purpose of the model** is to learn how to reverse the steps—going from noisy to clear—by learning to predict the noise that was added in each step. The model starts by trying to estimate the noise that was added in the last step and subtracting it. Then, it moves to the previous step, subtracts more noise, and so on, gradually reconstructing the original cat image.

In practice, this reverse process involves a **Markov chain**, where each step depends only on the previous one. Over many iterations, the model learns to generate entirely new images from noise—images that were not part of the training data but are consistent with what it has learned about the structure of cats.

Example 2: Image Denoising

Imagine you have a grainy photograph taken in low light conditions. **Diffusion models** can remove that noise and restore the image to a more realistic, sharper version. Image denoising is critical in industries like satellite imaging, where raw satellite images often contain noise due to atmospheric interference, or medical imaging (like MRI or CT scans), where noise can obscure important details.

In these cases, the diffusion model learns the statistical properties of noise in the data and removes it step by step, revealing a more precise image. For example, in **Denoising Diffusion Probabilistic Models (DDPMs)**, a model is trained on a high-volume dataset of clean images and their noisy versions. The model becomes proficient at removing noise from new, unseen images by learning the transition from noise to clarity.

Example 3: Molecular Structure Simulation

Diffusion models also find applications in fields like **computational chemistry**, where they simulate molecular structures. Here, noise represents the stochastic nature of atomic movements and interactions. By modeling the denoising process, the diffusion model can predict the arrangement of atoms in molecules based on partial, noisy data.

For example, in drug discovery, researchers often have incomplete data about a molecule's structure due to limitations in experimental measurements (e.g., X-ray crystallography). A diffusion model can take the noisy, incomplete structure and generate a more refined, realistic model of the molecule's atomic arrangement. This accelerates the design of new compounds by providing more accurate starting points for simulations, reducing the need for expensive and time-consuming laboratory experiments. Diffusion models stand out for their ability to generate high-fidelity results, especially in domains where maintaining intricate details is crucial. Their use of noise as a primary factor in learning and generating data makes them uniquely powerful for applications requiring precision and subtle refinement, from art creation and photography to scientific research in chemistry and medicine.

Variational Autoencoders (VAEs)

Variational Autoencoders (VAEs) are built to transform data into a compressed latent space before reconstructing it back to the original data format. The term "variational" highlights the model's capability to introduce an element of randomness or variation during this encoding and decoding process. VAEs are particularly useful when you want to produce varied outputs from a limited dataset. At the heart of a VAE are two critical components:

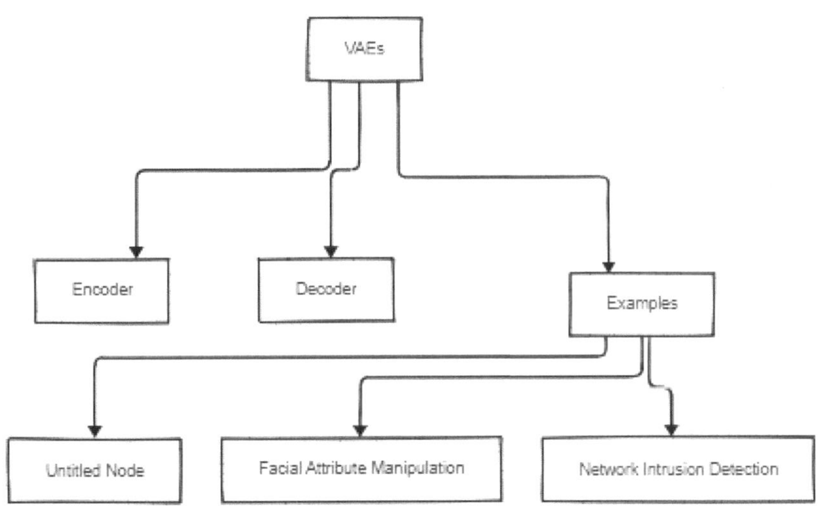

Fig 1.2 Variational Autoencoders (VAEs) with key components and examples

This image illustrates the structure of Variational Autoencoders (VAEs). At the top of the diagram, the central node labeled "VAEs" branches out into three key components:

"Encoder" on the left, "Decoder" in the middle, and "Examples" on the right. Each of these components further branches out to represent specific elements or applications. Under the "Encoder" node, there is a placeholder box labeled "Untitled Node." The "Examples" node branches out to two specific applications of VAEs: "Facial Attribute Manipulation" and "Network Intrusion Detection."

The Encoder

The encoder transforms high-dimensional input data, such as images, text samples, or numerical sequences, into a more manageable lower-dimensional latent space. This latent space serves as a streamlined, abstract representation of the original data, effectively capturing its core features while eliminating unnecessary details. For instance, consider a dataset of customer reviews for a product. Each review may contain thousands of words, resulting in a high-dimensional representation with numerous features. The encoder reduces this data to a 2D or 3D latent space, where each point's position captures essential sentiments or themes expressed in the reviews, such as positivity or negativity while discarding less relevant words and phrases However, 'variational' adds an important dimension to this process. Instead of assigning each input directly to a specific point in the latent space, the encoder assigns it to a distribution, typically a Gaussian (normal) distribution. This approach means that for every input, the encoder generates two vectors: one representing the mean (μ) and the other representing the latent variable's standard deviation (σ). By sampling from this distribution, the model incorporates an element of randomness into the representation. This characteristic enables Variational Autoencoders (VAEs) to produce a range of diverse outputs from the same input.

The Decoder

After the encoder has transformed the data into the latent space, the decoder takes on the next task. Its responsibility is to reconstruct the original data from the sampled latent variables. Essentially, the decoder maps the points in the latent space back to the original high-dimensional space, such as recreating the 28x28 pixel image of a handwritten digit. One of the key benefits of VAEs is that by sampling from the latent space distribution, they can generate multiple different outputs from the same general region of space. **For example**, if you sample near the region corresponding to the digit "3," the decoder might generate several slightly different versions of the number three, each with different thicknesses, orientations, or styles. This capability makes VAEs useful in applications where you want to generate a range of diverse outputs, not just one specific reconstruction. One of the classic uses of VAEs is anomaly detection, particularly in domains where normal behavior can be compressed into a latent space, and anomalies manifest as deviations from that space.

Example: Network Intrusion Detection

Consider a network monitoring system that tracks thousands of events per second. In this case, "normal" behavior is typically repetitive and predictable—most network traffic follows well-defined patterns. A VAE can be trained on standard traffic data, compressing it into a latent space that captures these regular patterns.Once trained, the VAE can process incoming network events in real time. If the VAE can encode and decode a network event with minimal reconstruction error (i.e., the output closely resembles the input), the event is classified as usual. However, if an event produces a high reconstruction error (i.e., the VAE struggles to reconstruct it), it is flagged as an anomaly. This might indicate an intrusion or unusual activity that deviates from the learned normal behavior. The randomness introduced in the latent space also makes VAEs more robust against overfitting to the standard data—meaning they are better at generalizing to unseen patterns. VAEs also shine in image generation, where the goal is to generate multiple variations of an object or scene from a learned distribution.

Example: Facial Attribute Manipulation

Imagine a dataset of facial images where you want to generate new faces with varying attributes—such as different expressions, ages, or hairstyles. A VAE trained on this dataset compresses each face into a point in the latent space. The interesting part comes from manipulating this latent space. **For example**, moving along one dimension in the latent space can modify specific facial attributes, like turning a smile into a frown. Another dimension might correspond to aging the face or changing the hair color. By sampling from different parts of the latent space and tweaking these dimensions, you can generate a wide range of facial images with slight variations in expression, age, and style.

Balancing Reconstruction and Randomness

One of the core technical challenges in VAEs is finding the right balance between reconstruction accuracy and variability. The encoder-decoder pair is trained to minimize two things:

Reconstruction Loss - This metric evaluates the decoder's effectiveness in recreating the original data from the latent space. If the Variational Autoencoder (VAE) prioritizes variability at the expense of accuracy, the generated outputs may appear blurry or distorted.

Kullback-Leibler (KL) Divergence Loss assesses the similarity between the learned distribution of the latent space and a standard normal distribution. This component motivates the Variational Autoencoder (VAE) to incorporate sufficient randomness in the latent space, fostering the generation of diverse outputs while maintaining a well-organized distribution. A well-trained VAE balances these two objectives: it produces outputs similar enough to the input to be recognizable but different enough to capture the natural variability of the data.

Generative Adversarial Networks

Generative Adversarial Networks (GANs) are powerful yet intricate models in machine learning. They work through a dynamic interaction between two neural networks: the generator, which creates data, and the discriminator, which evaluates its authenticity. As these two networks interact, the generator progressively enhances its output, learning to create increasingly realistic data through a training process that involves competing with the discriminator.

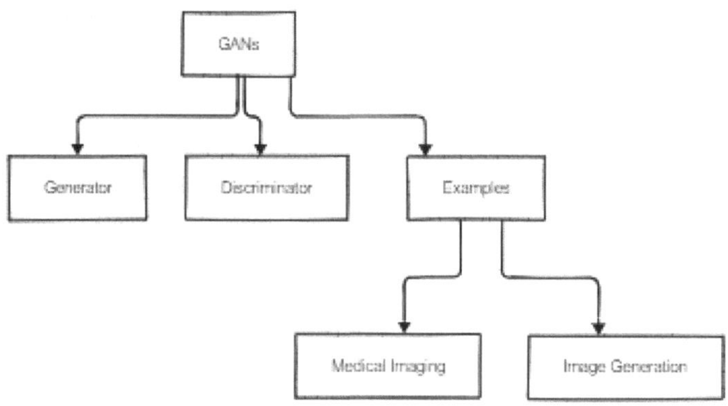

Fig 1.3 Generative Adversarial Networks (GANs) with key components and examples.

This image depicts the structure of Generative Adversarial Networks (GANs). At the top of the diagram, the central node labeled "GANs" branches out into three main components: "Generator" on the left, "Discriminator" in the middle, and "Examples" on the right. Each of these components further branches out to represent specific elements or applications. The "Generator" and "Discriminator" nodes are connected directly to the central GANs node, highlighting their roles as the two core components of GANs. The "Examples" node branches out to two specific applications of GANs: "Medical Imaging" and "Image Generation."

To better understand this, let us walk through a more concrete example **generation** using GANs.

Imagine a GAN tasked with generating high-resolution human faces. The **generator** starts with random noise and uses this noise to create a low-quality image that vaguely resembles a human face. This early image might look like a rough sketch, with distorted features and unnatural colors. The **discriminator**, trained on thousands of real human faces, will quickly detect that this image is fake and provide feedback.

In each training cycle, the generator refines its method by learning from the feedback provided by the discriminator. The feedback loop leads to gradual improvements in the generated images. Over time, the generator learns to recreate features like skin texture, lighting, and facial expressions. After enough iterations, the images produced by the generator can be nearly indistinguishable from real human faces. This is the same process used in **deepfake** technology, where GANs are trained to produce hyper-realistic videos by synthesizing facial movements, expressions, and even voices to create convincing but entirely fake media. Another robust use case for GANs is in medical imaging. In scenarios where obtaining authentic medical images is difficult due to privacy concerns or the scarcity of certain data types (such as rare diseases), GANs can be used to generate synthetic images. For instance, a GAN could be trained to produce high-quality MRI or CT scans, which can then be used to augment training datasets for machine learning models. This is invaluable for developing diagnostic tools, especially in areas where annotated medical data is complex. The process follows a repeated cycle: the generator creates synthetic images, and the discriminator evaluates them by comparing them to accurate medical scans. This adversarial training enables the generator to refine its ability to create realistic scans that reflect the intricacies and details found in genuine medical images.

Transformer Networks

Transformers have revolutionized generative AI, particularly in natural language processing (NLP) and text generation tasks. Unlike traditional recurrent neural networks (RNNs), which process data sequentially, transformers can handle entire data sequences in parallel. This is achieved through a mechanism called self-attention, where the model evaluates the relationship between different parts of the data sequence at the same time.

The Self-Attention Mechanism: A Game-Changer for Contextual Understanding

The fundamental advancement in transformers lies in the self-attention mechanism, which allows the model to concurrently evaluate the significance of various elements within a sequence. This capability addresses a key challenge encountered by recurrent neural networks (RNNs) and extended short-term memory networks (LSTMs): managing long-range dependencies. In these traditional models, information from the earlier segments of a sequence can become "forgotten" or lose its relevance as the model continues to process subsequent elements. Consequently, this limitation hampers performance, mainly when there are strong connections between the beginning and end of a sequence, such as in lengthy text passages.

Unlike traditional approaches, self-attention enables the model to simultaneously consider every word in a sequence, allowing for dynamic adjustments in how words influence one another. This capability is especially beneficial for tasks such as text generation and translation, where the meaning of a word can be shaped by context that may be several words away. For instance, in machine translation, the term 'bank' in the sentence 'She sat on the bank' can denote either a financial institution or the edge of a river, depending on the surrounding context. The self-attention mechanism empowers the model to discern the correct meaning by analyzing all words about each other rather than relying solely on their proximity. Consider a technical document with the following paragraph: "Cloud computing offers scalable resources over the internet, allowing businesses to adjust their computing needs on-demand. This flexibility can generate significant cost savings, as organizations only pay for the resources they consume. Additionally, cloud services provide robust security measures and disaster recovery options to ensure data integrity and availability." If we wanted to generate a summary of this paragraph, a Recurrent Neural Network (RNN) might process each sentence sequentially. It begins by reading "Cloud computing offers scalable resources over the internet" and gradually builds context as it processes each subsequent sentence. This method can be limited due to memory constraints and its sequential nature, which makes it slow and less efficient for understanding long-range dependencies. In contrast, a transformer model processes the entire paragraph simultaneously. Using self-attention mechanisms, it evaluates the relationships between all words and phrases at once, determining that key concepts like "scalable resources," "on-demand," "cost savings," "security measures," and "disaster recovery" are crucial. This parallel processing allows the transformer to handle long documents and efficiently capture long-range dependencies. The transformer can then generate a coherent summary that encapsulates the main points: "Cloud computing provides scalable, on-demand resources that lead to cost savings and offer robust security and disaster recovery options." This demonstrates how transformers, with their ability to process text in parallel and focus on important elements, offer significant advantages over RNNs in tasks like document summarization, making them a powerful tool for managing and understanding technical documentation.

Positional Encoding: Giving Structure to Sequence

One of the transformers' fundamental challenges, due to their parallel processing, is the loss of sequence order information. In traditional RNNs and LSTMs, the order of words or tokens is naturally preserved due to their sequential nature. However, transformers address this issue with positional encoding—a technique that embeds positional information into each token, ensuring the model knows the relative positions of words within a sentence.

The positional encoding adds sine and cosine functions to the word embeddings, ensuring the model understands where each word appears in the sequence. For example, in the sentence "The dog chased the ball," positional encoding ensures that "dog" comes before "ball," which is critical for understanding the meaning. Without positional information, the model might confuse the order and generate incorrect or illogical outputs.

Example: Music Generation

In music generation, transformer models can also take advantage of positional encoding. For instance, when generating a piece of music, the order of notes and their relationships are crucial for creating harmonious melodies. A transformer can consider the entire composition simultaneously, while positional encodings ensure that the notes follow a logical progression—resulting in coherent and melodious outputs rather than random noise.

Transformer Applications: From Text to Code, Music, and Beyond

Transformer models are not only limited to text generation tasks. Their versatility comes from their ability to handle any data represented as sequences, which opens various applications across different domains.

Text Summarization: In text summarization, transformers can generate concise summaries by identifying the most important components of the input text. By leveraging self-attention, transformers focus on the key parts that best represent the meaning of the entire document, producing informative and concise summaries. This capability is used in business analytics tools, where documents such as reports or legal contracts must be summarized automatically.

Machine Translation: Transformers are the backbone of modern translation services like Google Translate. When translating a sentence from English to French, for example, a transformer examines the entire sentence simultaneously, identifying how words in English relate to their French counterparts based on local and global context. This allows for more accurate translations than older, sequential models that might lose track of long-distance dependencies or word order.

Code Generation: Transformer models have generated programming code based on natural language descriptions. For instance, OpenAI's Codex—based on GPT—can translate a problem description like "write a function that reverses a string" into Python code.

Music Generation: In music generation, transformer models analyze musical sequences to predict the following notes in a melody or composition. For example, MuseNet, a transformer-based model, can generate classical symphonies, jazz compositions, or even pop music by processing musical notes as sequential data. Positional encoding ensures that the generated music follows rhythmic structures, and self-attention ensures that notes are harmonically related across the entire piece.

Image Captioning: Another robust use case of transformers is in image captioning, where the model generates textual descriptions of images. By processing the entire image as a sequence of visual tokens and combining it with text data, the model can generate detailed captions like "A brown dog is playing with a ball in the park." This is particularly useful in accessibility applications, where images need to be described for visually impaired users.

Conclusion

Generative AI has ushered in a new era of technological innovation, much like the invention of the printing press or the dawn of the internet. From its early days with ELIZA to the sophisticated models we see today, such as ChatGPT, GANs, VAEs, Diffusion Models, and Transformers, generative AI has evolved in leaps and bounds. It is akin to watching a toddler grow into a master artist, gaining skills and finesse with each passing year. This chapter peeled back the layers of generative AI, revealing the historical milestones, technological advancements, and core principles driving this field forward. We explored the tumultuous journey through the AI winters, where optimism waned, but valuable lessons were learned, setting the stage for today's breakthroughs. We delved into key architectures like GANs, which thrive on a creative rivalry between a generator and a discriminator, and Transformers, which have revolutionized text processing with their ability to understand context in parallel.

Generative AI's power lies in its ability to mimic human creativity and its potential to augment our own, opening new horizons for innovation and collaboration. As we look to the future, the applications of generative AI seem boundless, offering the promise of more innovative, more intuitive tools that can help us solve complex problems and enhance our creative endeavors. By understanding these foundational concepts and historical contexts, you are better equipped to engage with the transformative world of generative AI, whether you want to apply it in your projects or appreciate the incredible advancements in this exciting field.

Exercise: Test Your Understanding

Answer the following questions and test your understanding of learning from

`Chapter 1`:

`Q. 1.` How can generative AI enhance creativity in art, music, and writing? Provide specific examples.

`Q. 2.` How did the introduction of transformer architecture revolutionize natural language processing (NLP), and what are some real-world applications?

`Q. 3.` Explain the concept of Generative Adversarial Networks (GANs) and provide an example of their application?

`Q. 4.` Explain the significance of the self-attention mechanism in transformer networks.

`Q. 5.` How can generative AI enhance creativity in art, music, and writing? Provide specific examples.

2

Navigating Language Models

The first time I found myself at the intersection of the Large Language Model and real-world business problems was not because of a shiny new tool or the latest trend in AI. It was while working on a procurement hub solution for a multinational. The hub was designed to centralize sourcing, contract management, and supplier insights across regions, but the scale was massive. Data from thousands of contracts, compliance documents, and supplier communications flowed daily.

At the core of the procurement hub's struggle was an issue that traditional AI had long wrestled with **understanding and interpreting unstructured data**. Traditional AI models, despite their sophistication, were like expert rule-followers. They could categorize information, flag keywords, and apply predefined logic. However, the complexity of procurement—where contract clauses are phrased in multiple ways and supplier terms vary across regions and industries—proved too dynamic for conventional AI approaches. We used rule-based systems that worked well for structured data like invoices and purchase orders. However, these systems hit their limits regarding contract language, compliance variations, and supplier negotiations.

Consider a scenario: You are dealing with a supplier who promises a discount for early payments, but the contract buries this under vague, legalistic terms. Traditional AI could tell you something related to payments, but it would not know how to identify the specific condition or bring it to the forefront without clear, pre-programmed rules. Worse yet, if the language varied across different contracts, AI models would often miss critical details, leading to compliance risks and missed opportunities.

That is where the concept of language models (LLMs) stepped in and flipped the script. Instead of relying on manually created rules or rigid programming, Language models like GPT could interpret language as humans do. These models were not just reacting to keywords but understanding the context. The breakthrough was their ability to process vast amounts of natural language and grasp nuances in contracts, communications, and procurement data that traditional AI would struggle with.

However, not all language models are created equal. Depending on the task, the choice between **Large Language Models (LLMs)** and **Small Language Models (SLMs)** can significantly impact performance, efficiency, and cost. Choosing between LLMs and

SLMs depends on the task, much like selecting a precision screwdriver versus a heavy-duty drill. Each has its strengths, limitations, and best-fit applications.

This chapter delves into language models, exploring the fundamental differences between LLMs and SLMs, their respective strengths and limitations, and the practical applications where each excels. By the end of this chapter, readers will understand how to navigate the landscape of language models and make informed decisions about which model to use for specific tasks.

Large Language Model (LLM)

Large Language Models (LLMs) are advanced deep-learning models designed to process and understand natural language at an impressive scale. These models are pre-trained on vast datasets, enabling them to grasp language, context, and meaning complexities.

The magic behind LLMs lies in how they interpret context, thanks to their foundational architecture—transformers. Unlike traditional AI models, which rely heavily on predefined rules or simple pattern recognition, LLMs use **self-attention mechanisms** to focus on the relationships between words in a sentence, no matter how far apart. This ability to understand context and long-range dependencies in language became a game-changer for industries like procurement, where the meaning often depends on how terms are related across an entire document.

The foundation of the large model lies in the Transformer architecture, which fundamentally changed the landscape of natural language processing (NLP). It was designed to handle sequential data—like sentences in a document—without relying on recurrent neural networks (RNNs) or convolutional neural networks (CNNs).

The core of Transformer architecture lies in its self-attention mechanism. It allows the model to evaluate the importance of each word relative to every other word in the sequence, making it highly effective in understanding context. Here is a step-by-step breakdown of how self-attention works and practical examples to make it more relatable.

- **Input Representation**: Each word in a sentence is transformed into a vector through an embedding layer, which converts the words into a numerical format that the model can understand.
- **Creating Query, Key, and Value Vectors**: For each word vector xix_ixi, three different vectors are created:
    - **Query Vector**: This represents what the current word is looking for in the context of the entire sentence.
    - **Key Vector**: This represents the context that other words provide.

    - **Value Vector**: This contains the information the model will use to produce the output.
- **Calculating Attention Scores**: The self-attention mechanism calculates scores by performing a dot product between the query vector and each key vector. The resulting scores indicate how much focus to place on other words when interpreting the current word. After calculating these scores, a SoftMax function is applied to produce a probability distribution, which helps normalize the scores.
- **Weighting Values**: The self-attention layer produces an output by calculating a weighted sum of the value vectors, with the weights determined by the attention scores. This means the model can selectively gather information from the entire sentence based on the computed relevance of each word.

Consider the following sentence related to a project plan:

"The team will complete the project by the end of Q2."

Here is how self-attention would work in this scenario:

- **Input Representation**: Each word in the sentence is represented as a vector. For instance:
    - ""They"" might have a vector representation that captures its role as a determiner.
    - The "team" would have a vector that emphasizes the collective group responsible for the project.
- **Creating Query, Key, and Value Vectors**:
    - For the word "complete":
        - **Query Vector**: This vector seeks information about what will be completed (in this case, the project).
        - **Key Vector**: Other words, such as "team" and "project," will provide context about "complete."
        - **Value Vector**: This vector carries information about the project's completion, such as timelines.
- **Calculating Attention Scores**:
    - When processing the word "complete," the model evaluates how relevant each other word is to this action.
    - The word "team" will likely receive a high score since it indicates who is responsible for completing the project, while "the" would receive a low score as it does not provide substantive context.
- **Weighting Values**:
    - The model combines the information based on the attention scores. In this case, it might give more weight to "team" and "project" while downplaying "by" or "the."
    - The final output will emphasize that the **team** is leading in completing the **project**.

As we delve deeper into large language models (LLMs), it is essential to address the attributes that define their capabilities, their size and the challenges that come with it. The "large" in LLMs is not just a marketing term; it reflects a fundamental shift in how we approach natural language processing (NLP) and AI more broadly.

When we talk about LLMs, we generally refer to models with billions, even trillions, of parameters. Parameters are the weights and biases within the model that determine how it processes information. The sheer scale of these parameters allows LLMs to capture a vast array of patterns and nuances in language.

What is a Parameter?

To understand the significance of size, let us first clarify the parameters. In a neural network, parameters are the elements that get adjusted during training. Every parameter shapes the model's behavior and contributes to its ability to learn from the input data. The more parameters a model has, the more nuanced its understanding can be, akin to a musician mastering various techniques to play a complex piece of music.

The Impact of Size on Performance

The scale of LLMs leads to a range of benefits, particularly in their ability to generate high-quality text and comprehend context over long passages. For example, models like GPT-3 or GPT-4 can generate fluent human-like text that stays relevant to the topic across several paragraphs, a level of performance that smaller models often struggle to match. This increased size enables the model to remember more context, allowing it to carry on conversations or generate text that aligns closely with previous statements, much like how a skilled conversationalist maintains the flow of dialogue.

However, this size is not without its challenges. The vast parameters that grant LLMs their power also introduce a host of complexities that need to be managed:

Resource Intensive

Training LLMs requires substantial computational resources. The process can be incredibly energy-intensive, often demanding specialized hardware such as GPUs or TPUs (Tensor Processing Units). This resource requirement incurs high costs and raises concerns about the environmental impact of training such large models.

Inference Time and Latency

Once trained, deploying LLMs can also present challenges. Their size often results in longer inference times—the time it takes for the model to generate a response after receiving input. This latency can be critical in practical applications, especially scenarios requiring real-time responses, such as customer service bots or interactive applications.

Fine-Tuning and Adaptability

Another significant challenge is fine-tuning LLMs for specific tasks. While these models are powerful in their general capabilities, they may not perform optimally out of the box for niche applications. Fine-tuning requires additional data, time, and cost, complicating the implementation process.

Ethical Considerations

The deployment of LLMs also brings ethical considerations to the forefront. Larger models can inadvertently amplify biases present in their training data, leading to the generation of prejudiced or harmful content. Ensuring ethical AI use involves refining these models, being vigilant about their outputs, and establishing frameworks for responsible AI use.

Understanding and Interpretability

Despite their impressive capabilities, LLMs often operate as "black boxes," making it difficult to understand how they arrive at specific outputs. This lack of interpretability can be a barrier in critical fields like healthcare or finance, where understanding the rationale behind decisions is paramount. Developers must grapple with the challenge of creating explainable AI systems that can clarify how and why certain decisions are made. Given the multifaceted challenges associated with LLMs, organizations are increasingly exploring alternative approaches to address their specific needs. This is where Small Language Models (SLMs) come into play. While LLMs shine in their ability to handle vast amounts of data and generate intricate outputs, SLMs offer a different set of advantages that can make them more suitable for specific applications.

Small Language Models (SLMs)

A Small Language Model (SLM) is a computational model designed to understand and generate natural language, like its larger counterparts, but on a more focused and efficient scale. SLMs are tailored for specific natural language processing tasks, offering valuable functionality while requiring significantly less computational power. SLMs are built using simplified versions of the neural network architecture found in LLMs. SLMs typically contain fewer parameters than their larger counterparts, often in the millions rather than billions. While this reduced size means they may lack the extensive capabilities of LLMs, SLMs can be more efficient, faster, and easier to deploy in specific scenarios. SLMs are typically trained on smaller, domain-specific datasets. This targeted approach ensures that the model excels in the specific tasks it was designed for without requiring the vast computational resources necessary to train an LLM.

Key Benefits of Small Language Models

SLMs provide several advantages that make them ideal for many real-world applications:

- **Efficiency** With fewer parameters and a more minor architecture, SLMs require less computational power and memory. This makes them suitable for deployment on devices with limited resources, such as mobile phones, edge devices, or legacy systems.
- **Speed** Due to their lightweight nature, SLMs offer faster inference times. This means they can process and generate responses more quickly than larger models. This speed is critical in real-time applications like chatbots and customer support systems.
- **Cost-Effectiveness** Training and deploying an SLM is significantly more affordable than an LLM. Organizations that need to perform specific NLP tasks can achieve their goals without incurring the high costs associated with large-scale models.
- **Domain-Specific Excellence** SLMs are highly effective in specialized contexts where the range of language patterns is limited and well-defined. Their training can focus on specific industries, such as legal, medical, or financial sectors, ensuring accurate and contextually relevant outputs.

Specific Use Cases for SLMs

In this section, we will discuss relevant Use-Cases for SLMs.

Automotive Industry: Vehicle Diagnostics and Support

In the automotive sector, SLMs can be employed in vehicle diagnostic systems. Decision-making must often occur in real time, where milliseconds can be crucial. For instance, an SLM could be deployed locally within the vehicle's onboard system to interpret voice commands from the driver, process environmental data, or manage basic navigation tasks.

Another scenario can be when a driver encounters an issue with their vehicle; they can interact with an SLM-based virtual assistant. For example, A driver experiencing engine troubles can describe the symptoms, such as unusual noises or warning lights. SLM can quickly analyze these inputs against a database of standard vehicle issues and provide a set of likely diagnoses, suggesting potential fixes or indicating when professional service is necessary.

Remote Operations in Mining or Oil Fields

In mining or oil extraction industries, sites are often located in remote areas where internet connectivity is unreliable or non-existent. Deploying SLMs can facilitate essential operations without relying on cloud resources.

Workers in the field can use SLMs for natural language queries related to operational guidelines or safety protocols, ensuring immediate access to critical information even without internet connectivity.

Sensitive Healthcare Data

An SLM trained in specific medical datasets can understand and generate responses using precise medical terminology. For example, if a healthcare professional queries about drug interactions, an SLM can provide tailored information without needing to retrain a larger LLM, which may not have been fine-tuned for that specific medical context.

Advantages of Small Language Models (SLMs)

Building on these scenarios, let us explore the advantages of deploying SLMs in contexts where they outshine LLMs:

- **Efficiency and Speed** Due to their smaller size, SLMs often exhibit quicker inference times, allowing for real-time applications without the latency issues that can affect LLMs. This speed is essential in autonomous vehicles or remote operations, where split-second decisions can be critical.
- **Resource Accessibility** Training and deploying SLMs require significantly less computational power, making them more accessible to organizations with limited resources. For instance, mining companies or rural healthcare facilities can leverage SLMs without the heavy infrastructure costs associated with LLMs.
- **Simplicity and Focus** SLMs can be designed for specific tasks, allowing them to perform exceptionally well in narrow domains. In healthcare, for example, a model tailored for interpreting patient symptoms can deliver improved performance compared to a more generalized LLM.
- **Data Sensitivity and Compliance** In sensitive data scenarios, SLMs can operate

locally, ensuring that information does not leave the device and thus minimize the risk of data breaches. This local process is critical for maintaining confidentiality and compliance with data protection regulations for legal and healthcare applications.

- **Cost-Effectiveness** Fine-tuning a large LLM to handle specialized language or sensitive data can be resource-intensive and costly. In contrast, SLMs can be developed with specific training datasets focusing on the required domain, resulting in a more efficient and cost-effective solution. For instance, rather than investing in extensive fine-tuning of an LLM for legal jargon, a law firm can deploy an SLM specifically trained on legal documents, saving time and resources.

Challenges Faced by SLMs

Despite their advantages, SLMs also come with challenges that organizations must consider:

Limited Generalization

While SLMs excel in specific, narrow tasks, their ability to generalize across diverse applications is often limited. Generalization refers to a model's capability to apply learned patterns to new, unseen data or different contexts. SLMs may not possess the extensive training or broad dataset exposure that LLMs have, resulting in challenges such as:

- **Contextual Limitations**: SLMs may struggle to comprehend complex contexts that require nuanced understanding or reasoning. For example, in legal settings, a phrase could have different meanings based on the context of a case. An SLM might miss subtle differences or implications, leading to incorrect conclusions.
- **Performance Variability**: When applied to a domain outside their training focus, SLMs can produce outputs that lack accuracy or relevance. For example, in a scenario where an SLM is tasked with processing customer feedback across multiple product lines, it may perform well for one line but poorly for another due to its narrow training scope.

Data Requirements

To achieve adequate performance, SLMs require high-quality training data tailored to their specific tasks. The challenges associated with data requirements include:

- **Quality over Quantity**: While LLMs can leverage vast datasets to improve their capabilities, SLMs depend on high-quality, domain-specific data. Collecting such data can be labor-intensive and costly. For example, a healthcare SLM trained to interpret medical records must have access to annotated medical data to ensure accuracy.
- **Time-Consuming Curation**: Gathering and curating this high-quality data can be

Feature	SLM	LLM
Speed	Faster due to minor architecture	Slower due to computational demands
Resource Needs	Minimal, can be used for edge devices as well	High, requiring advanced hardware
Accuracy	High in narrow domains	High in diverse and complex tasks

Here is a comparison summary:

Complementary Nature of LLMs and SLMs

Understanding the complementary nature of LLMs and SLMs is key to leveraging their strengths effectively. Here is how organizations can balance the two:

- **Hybrid Approaches** businesses can adopt hybrid models that combine the capabilities of both LLMs and SLMs. For instance, an LLM can handle more complex, nuanced queries, while SLMs manage simpler, more straightforward tasks. This segmentation allows for an optimized workflow that maximizes efficiency.

  To better understand, let us revisit our procurement hub.

  - **LLMs in Action**: LLMs became indispensable when dealing with a corpus of thousands of contracts in various formats and languages. They could interpret legal clauses, extract obligations, and flag risks—even when the phrasing varied drastically. Their ability to generalize across vast datasets made them perfect for tasks like:
    - **Contract Analysis**: Identifying clauses related to penalties, discounts, or obligations without predefined rules.
    - **Supplier Insights**: Analysing communication patterns to detect risks or opportunities.
    - **Multilingual Compliance**: Translating and analyzing documents across global regions seamlessly.

- **SLMs in Action**: For smaller, targeted tasks, SLMs offered a lightweight, efficient alternative. Need to auto-process invoices or provide onboarding support to the suppliers? SLMs could handle these with speed and accuracy, consuming fewer resources. Their strengths included:

    - Invoice Processing: SLMs can validate invoices by analyzing key details such as PO numbers, amounts, and due dates, cross-checking them against predefined rules or the procurement system, and flagging inconsistencies.

    - Customizable Procurement Chatbots: SLMs can power lightweight procurement chatbots that handle FAQs, assist suppliers with onboarding queries, or guide users through procurement processes like submitting a new purchase request or tracking an order

- **Task Suitability** choosing between LLMs and SLMs often depends on the specific task at hand. LLMs may be the better choice for tasks requiring deep contextual understanding or creative text generations such as drafting long-form articles. In contrast, while SLMs may not have the same level of complexity as LLMs, they can effectively generate text and perform more straightforward tasks. Models like Phi-3 showcase the capabilities of SLMs in generating relevant and contextually appropriate text for specific applications.

- **Cost-Effectiveness** implementing a combination of LLMs and SLMs can lead to more cost-effective solutions. Organizations can allocate resources where needed, using LLMs for high-value tasks and SLMs for routine functions, resulting in a more sustainable operational model.

Conclusion

In summary, while Small Language Models (SLMs) offer significant advantages in speed, efficiency, and cost-effectiveness, they also present challenges such as limited generalization, stringent data requirements, and the risk of overfitting. By understanding these challenges and leveraging the complementary nature of both LLMs and SLMs, organizations can develop effective strategies that optimize language models based on specific needs and contexts.

Exercise: Test Your Understanding

Answer the following questions and test your understanding of learning from

`Chapter 2`:

`Q. 1.` How can organizations leverage the complementary strengths of LLMs and SLMs to foster innovation and maintain competitive advantage in rapidly evolving industries?

`Q. 2.` How might integrating LLMs and SLMs shift the balance of power in industries heavily reliant on nuanced language interpretation, such as legal or medical sectors?

`Q. 3.` How do SLMs compare to LLMs in real-world business applications?

`Q. 4.` What are the biggest challenges when deploying SLMs?

`Q. 5.` How do SLMs impact AI adoption in cost-sensitive industries like manufacturing and retail?

Master the Basics Before the Magic

Take time to understand the foundational concepts — like neural networks, tokenization, and transformer architecture — before diving into prompt engineering.

3

Introduction to Vector Databases

Data is everywhere, growing by the second, far outpacing our ability to organize, understand, and use it effectively. Over the past decade, businesses, scientists, and technologists have grappled with a fundamental challenge: How do you make sense of data that does not neatly fit into rows and columns? Search engines struggled to go beyond keyword matches, often missing the nuance of what users were looking for. Constrained by rigid categorical data, recommendation systems made generic suggestions rather than meaningful ones. Machine learning models spent excessive time wrestling with the limits of traditional databases, which were never built to process the diverse, unstructured data we now generate—text, images, audio, and beyond. The problem was not just size. It was complex. Data was becoming messier, richer, and more interconnected. Think of a single photo: it is not just a JPEG file; it carries colors, objects, scenes, emotions, and context. Traditional databases could not capture or leverage these intricate patterns. The same was true for legal documents, customer feedback, or a collection of songs—each full of hidden relationships that linear storage systems could not reveal.

The Emergence of Vector Databases

Vector databases arose to meet the growing demand for systems capable of storing data and understanding its underlying structure and relationships. Unlike traditional databases, which store data in rows and columns, vector databases represent information as high-dimensional vectors. This innovative design allows for nuanced analysis and pattern recognition, making them indispensable in modern applications such as semantic search, recommendation systems, machine learning, and generative artificial intelligence (AI). By clustering related data based on similarities, vector databases enhance the efficiency and intelligence of various computational tasks.

At the heart of this transformation are vector embeddings.

What Are Vector Embeddings?

Vector embeddings are numerical representations of data points in a multidimensional space that capture relationships, meanings, and contextual similarities. The fundamental idea is that similar items should have embeddings closer together, while dissimilar items should be farther apart. Most machine learning models cannot directly process raw data such as words, sentences, or images. Instead, they must be converted into numerical forms that preserve relationships and structures. Traditional representations (like one-hot encoding) are often sparse and inefficient, whereas vector embeddings provide a dense, continuous, and meaningful data representation.

For example, in NLP, embeddings help capture relationships such as:

- **Synonymy**: Words with similar meanings (e.g., "happy" and "joyful") have similar embeddings.
- **Contextual Meaning**: The meaning of a word changes depending on the sentence (e.g., "bank" in "river bank" vs. "bank account").
- **Analogies:** Relationships such as "King - Man + Woman ≈ Queen" can be modeled mathematically.

How Are Vector Embeddings Generated?

Different machine learning models generate embeddings based on the data type:

Word Embeddings (Text-Based Models)

For textual data, embeddings represent words or sentences in a way that captures their meaning. A word embedding is a low-dimensional vector representation of a word, learned so that similar words have similar vector values. These vectors are generated using deep learning or matrix factorization techniques. Words are mapped to a multidimensional space where similar words are positioned close to each other.

Example:

- "piano" → [0.21, -0.14, 0.87, -0.45, …]
- "guitar" → [0.23, -0.13, 0.85, -0.44, …]
- "airplane" → [-0.70, 0.90, 0.30, -0.60, …]

Here, "piano" and "guitar" have closer vector representations compared to "airplane," reflecting their semantic similarity as musical instruments.

Similarity Measures

Similarity measures can be used to compare two words. Several similarity measures can be used to calculate how close two vectors are in the embedding space.

Dot Product

The Dot Product is a fundamental mathematical operation widely used as a similarity measure in vector-based computations, including search, recommendation systems, and embeddings in vector databases. It quantifies the relationship between two vectors by considering their direction and magnitude, making it particularly useful in scenarios where both factors carry meaningful information.
Mathematically, the dot product of two vectors A and B (each with n dimensions) is computed as:

$$\text{dot product}(a,b) = |a| \times |b| \times \cos(\theta)$$

where $|\mathbf{a}|$ and $|\mathbf{b}|$ are the magnitudes (lengths) of the vectors, and θ is the angle between them.

This operation results in a single scalar value that provides insight into the orientation and scale of the vectors relative to each other:

- Positive values indicate the vectors are aligned in a similar direction, meaning they have a strong positive correlation.
- Negative values suggest that the vectors point opposite directions, implying an inverse relationship.
- A zero value signifies that the vectors are orthogonal (perpendicular) and share no directional similarity.

Cosine Similarity

Unlike the dot product, which considers both magnitude and direction, cosine similarity focuses only on the angle between two vectors, making it ideal for comparing the relative orientation of high-dimensional data points. Cosine similarity measures the angle between two vectors in a multidimensional space, disregarding their magnitudes. It is calculated as the inner product of the vectors divided by the product of their lengths, yielding a value that ranges from -1 to 1. For instance, identical vectors yield a cosine similarity of 1, orthogonal vectors result in 0, and opposite vectors produce a similarity of -1.

$$\text{Cosine similarity} = x.\,y \,/\, ||x|| \times ||y||$$

Where:

- $x\,.\,y$ = product (dot) of the vectors 'x' and 'y'.
- $||x||$ and $||y||$ = length (magnitude) of the two vectors 'x' and 'y'.
- $||x|| \times ||y||$ = regular product of the two vectors 'x' and 'y'.

- Closer words have a higher cosine similarity (closer to 1).
- Unrelated words have values near zero or negative.

Example:
- Cosine Similarity between ("dog", "cat") ≈ 0.95 (similar words).
- Cosine Similarity between ("dog", "car") ≈ 0.10 (unrelated words).
- Euclidean distance - Unlike dot product and cosine similarity, which assess directional similarity, Euclidean distance calculates the straight-line distance between two vectors in a multidimensional space. This makes it particularly useful in applications where the absolute positioning of vectors matters.

For two vectors A and B in an n-dimensional space, the Euclidean distance is given by:

$$d(A, B) = \sqrt{\sum_{i=1}^{n}(A_i - B_i)^2}$$

- Smaller values indicate that the vectors (or data points) are closer together.
- Larger values suggest that the vectors are farther apart.
    - Euclidean distance always returns a non-negative value with zero indicating identical vectors.

Similarity Measure	Considerations	Best Used For
Dot Product	Captures both magnitude and direction	Stock price movement, physics-based models
Cosine Similarity	Only considers direction (ignores magnitude)	NLP, recommendation systems
Euclidean Distance	Measures absolute distance in space	Image recognition, anomaly detection

Popular Models for Text Embedding

The following are the most widely used text embedding models, categorized by their type:

Word-Level Embedding Models

These models generate embeddings at the word level but do not consider the broader sentence context.

Word2Vec (Google, 2013)

Key Features:

- Uses two architectures:
  - Continuous Bag of Words (CBOW) – Predicts a word from its surrounding words.
  - Skip-Gram – Predicts surrounding words from a given word.
- Captures word similarity based on how words appear in context.

Example:

- "King – Man + Woman = Queen" (word vector arithmetic).

Pros:

- It is efficient and captures semantic relationships well.
- Works well for analogy tasks.

Cons:

- Cannot handle polysemy (multiple meanings of the same word).
- Fixed embeddings for words (i.e., "bank" in riverbank vs. financial bank is treated the same).

GloVe (Stanford, 2014)

Key Features:

- Uses word co-occurrence matrices to generate embeddings.
- Learns global statistics across the entire corpus, unlike Word2Vec, which focuses only on local context.
- Captures both syntactic and semantic relationships.

Pros:

- Works well for word similarity and analogies.
- It is more robust than Word2Vec in some cases.

Cons:

- Like Word2Vec, it does not handle word meaning variations in different contexts.

FastText (Facebook, 2016)

Key Features:

- Improves Word2Vec by representing words as sub word n-grams (e.g., "playing" → "play", "lay", "ayi", "ing").
- Can generate embeddings for unseen words (out-of-vocabulary or OOV words).

Pros:

- Handles rare words and misspellings better.
- Works well with morphologically rich languages like German, Finnish, and Turkish.

Cons:

- Requires more computation due to sub word processing.

Contextualized Embedding Models

These models generate embeddings based on sentence context, making them more potent than word-level embeddings.

BERT (Google, 2018)

Key Features:

- Stands for Bidirectional Encoder Representations from Transformers.
- Unlike previous models, BERT understands words in both the left and right contexts.
- Uses Masked Language Modelling (MLM) to train - randomly masks some words and predicts them.

Pros:

- Handles polysemy (e.g., "bank" has different vectors for "riverbank" vs. "money bank").
- Outperforms traditional models in NLP tasks (e.g., question answering, named entity recognition).

Cons:

- Computationally expensive.
- Outputs variable-length embeddings, making comparison difficult.

RoBERTa (Facebook, 2019)

Key Features:

- An optimized version of BERT with dynamic masking during training.
- Removes Next Sentence Prediction (NSP) from BERT, making it more efficient.
- Trained on a larger dataset for better generalization.

Pros:

- More robust than BERT in most NLP tasks.
- Better at sentence classification and ranking.

Cons:

- Computationally heavy, like BERT.

T5 (Google, 2019)

Key Features:

- Text-to-Text Transfer Transformer (T5) reformulates all NLP tasks into a text generation task.
- Example:
    - Sentiment analysis → "This movie is great." → "Positive"
    - Translation → "Translate English to French: Hello" → "Bonjour"

Pros:

- Extremely versatile across multiple NLP tasks.
- More effective in sequence-to-sequence problems.

Cons:

- The large model requires significant computing resources.

Sentence & Document Embedding Models

These models generate embeddings for entire sentences or documents, making them ideal for search, similarity, and retrieval tasks.

GPT Embeddings (text-embedding-ada-002, OpenAI, 2023)

Key Features:

- Best-in-class embeddings for search and retrieval-augmented Generation (RAG).
- Supports a 768-dimensional embedding space with exceptional performance.
- Used in ChatGPT, Microsoft Copilot, and AI search applications.

Pros:

- Extremely efficient and accurate for retrieval tasks.

- Optimized for semantic similarity.

Cons:

- Proprietary model (not open source).

Sentence-BERT (SBERT, 2019)

Key Features:

- A fine-tuned version of BERT for sentence similarity tasks.
- Uses Siamese & Triplet network architectures for better embedding quality.

Pros:

- Faster & more efficient for semantic similarity search.
- Works well with cosine similarity & clustering.

Cons:

- It is not as good as GPT embedding for long documents.

Storage and Indexing Mechanisms in Vector Databases

Vector databases are designed to store efficiently, index, and retrieve high-dimensional vectors, making them crucial for applications like machine learning, natural language processing (NLP), and image recognition. Their mechanisms ensure high-speed queries and effective management of complex data. Below is an exploration of how vector databases handle storage, indexing, and retrieval.

Vector Representation

Vectors are stored as arrays of numerical values, typically floating-point numbers, where each array element corresponds to a dimension in the vector space. This numerical representation allows for precise mathematical operations, such as distance or similarity computations.

- **Example**: In NLP, word embeddings like those introduced in Word2Vec (2013) or BERT (2019) represent words as 300-dimensional or higher vectors, capturing contextual relationships.

Indexing Techniques

To enable efficient vector retrieval, vector databases utilize sophisticated indexing methods tailored to high-dimensional data:

KD-Trees (1980s)

- Mechanism: KD-Trees partition the data space into hyper-rectangular regions based on vector dimensions. This method is effective for low-dimensional data but less for high-dimensional datasets due to the "curse of dimensionality."
- Example: Early computer vision tasks like image feature matching used KD-Trees to organize and search feature descriptors.

Ball Trees (1990s)

- Mechanism: Ball Trees partition data using hyperspheres, making them better suited for datasets with irregular distributions than KD-trees.
- Example: Image recognition systems use Ball Trees to organize feature vectors extracted from convolutional neural networks (CNNs).

Locality-Sensitive Hashing (LSH) (1998)

- Mechanism: LSH reduces the dimensionality of vectors while preserving relative distances, enabling faster searches.
- Example: Spotify uses LSH to recommend songs by finding tracks with similar audio features (e.g., tempo, timbre) to a user's favorite tracks.

Graph-Based Indexing (HNSW, 2016)

- Mechanism: Hierarchical Navigable Small World (HNSW) graphs create a network of nodes (vectors) and edges (distances), enabling fast approximate nearest neighbor searches.
- Example: OpenAI's embedding-based search uses HNSW graphs to retrieve semantically similar documents or code snippets.

Example of Popular Vector Database

FAISS (Facebook AI Similarity Search)

Developed by Meta (formerly Facebook AI), FAISS is an open-source library specializing in efficient similarity search and clustering dense vectors. Its design is optimized for high-dimensional spaces and supports CPU and GPU implementations.

Key Details:

Search Methods: FAISS offers an exact and approximate nearest neighbor (ANN) search, making it adaptable for varying latency and accuracy needs.

Indexing Techniques: It employs several indexing strategies (e.g., Inverted File Index (IVF), Product Quantization (PQ)) to balance search speed with memory usage.

Scalability: Designed for large-scale datasets, it can process millions of high-dimensional vectors, essential for image retrieval, document similarity, and

recommendation systems.
Performance: Its GPU support significantly accelerates search times, an advantage for real-time applications in machine learning pipelines.
Pinecone is a managed vector database service that abstracts away the complexities of deployment and scaling. It is built to deliver real-time vector search and similarity matching at scale with minimal operational overhead.

Key Details
Serverless Experience: As a managed service, Pinecone handles indexing, scaling, and infrastructure maintenance, allowing developers to focus on integrating vector search into their applications.

Hybrid Search: It supports combining vector-based similarity search with metadata filtering, making it a powerful tool for personal recommendations and semantic search.

Enterprise Integration: Its architecture is tailored for real-time applications like recommendation engines, chatbots, and search systems that leverage retrieval-augmented generation (RAG).

Ease of Use: Pinecone's API abstracts complex underlying algorithms, enabling rapid prototyping and deployment of vector-based applications without deep expertise in vector search mechanics.

Milvus is an open-source vector database designed for scalable similarity search and analytics of massive feature vectors. Developed by Zilliz, it is built to handle both structured and unstructured data in modern AI applications.

Indexing Variety: Milvus supports a range of ANN indexes, such as IVF, HNSW, and PQ, enabling customization based on dataset characteristics and performance requirements.

Cloud-Native Architecture: It is designed to be deployed in distributed environments, making it a strong choice for large-scale, cloud-based applications.
Versatility: Milvus is used in various applications—from facial recognition and voice search to document retrieval—thanks to its ability to integrate with existing data analytics frameworks.

Community & Support: As an open-source project, Milvus benefits from an active community and continuous updates, ensuring state-of-the-art performance.
Azure AI Search (Vector Search in Azure Cognitive Search)
Azure AI Search, part of Microsoft's Cognitive Search service, integrates vector search capabilities with traditional keyword-based search. This makes it a robust solution for enterprise-grade search scenarios requiring semantic and structured search

capabilities.

Hybrid Search Capabilities: Azure AI Search supports a hybrid approach, combining vector similarity search with conventional filtering and full-text search. This is particularly useful for enterprise applications that search across diverse data types (e.g., documents, images, metadata).

ANN Indexing: Leveraging algorithms such as Hierarchical Navigable Small World (HNSW) efficiently process high-dimensional vectors, enabling fast and accurate retrieval.

Enterprise-Ready: With built-in security, compliance, and scalability features, Azure AI Search is well-suited for large organizations and industries with strict regulatory requirements.

Integration Ecosystem: Seamlessly integrates with other Azure services (like Azure Machine Learning and OpenAI services), enabling developers to build sophisticated, end-to-end AI pipelines for applications such as customer support, legal document analysis, and multimodal search.

Applications of Vector Databases with Examples

Advanced Search and Semantic Relationships

- **Identifying Similar Entities**: Vector databases enable semantic searches by understanding the meaning behind data points rather than relying on exact matches. Example: In an e-commerce platform, when a user searches for "red shoes," the system can recommend items similar in style or color, such as burgundy or crimson sneakers, even if the tags differ from the query. In an image search, a vector database can identify images with similar visual features—such as specific textures, patterns, or objects—without requiring precise keywords.
- **Recommendation Systems**: Vector databases can deliver highly personalized recommendations by analyzing vectors representing user preferences and product attributes.

  Example: On a music streaming platform, if a user enjoys a calm acoustic track, the database can recommend other songs with similar tempos, moods, and instrumental arrangements, even if the genres differ. Similarly, based on viewers' past choices, Netflix can recommend shows with comparable storylines or themes.

Facilitating Machine Learning and Deep Learning

- **Efficient Data Clustering**: Vector databases simplify the process of preparing data for machine learning by clustering similar data points, making pattern recognition more effective.
  Example: In healthcare, a vector database can group patient data with similar symptoms and test results, allowing machine learning models to identify trends such as disease outbreaks or treatment efficacy.
- **Deep Learning Support**: Vector databases accelerate the retrieval of relevant high-dimensional data, which is essential for tasks requiring complex reasoning.
  Example: In autonomous driving, vector databases store and compare real-time sensor data (like LiDAR and camera inputs) with pre-stored data to detect obstacles or road patterns efficiently. In natural language processing, they help deep learning models like GPT-4 retrieve the most contextually relevant pieces of training data for better understanding and response generation.

Enhancing Large Language Models (LLMs) and Generative AI

- **Contextual Language Understanding**: Large language models utilize vector embeddings to store data and derive contextual meaning.
  Example: Suppose a user asks a virtual assistant, "What bark is good for health?" The vector database helps the assistant differentiate between tree bark (used in herbal remedies) and a dog's bark (irrelevant in this context), providing a precise response.
- **Generative AI Applications**: Vector databases enhance the capabilities of generative AI in producing creative outputs by associating and recombining similar data points.
  Example: When a user requests AI to generate a story about "a futuristic city with floating vehicles," the system retrieves and combines relevant concepts, such as futuristic architectural designs and transportation technologies, to craft a coherent narrative. The database identifies similar visual components in image generation, like metallic hues and sleek lines, to produce fitting imagery.

Below is a comprehensive comparison table summarizing key aspects of popular vector databases:

Vector Database	Developer/ Organization	Deployment Model	Key Features
FAISS	Facebook AI (Meta)	Open source; self-hosted with GPU support	- Supports both exact & approximate nearest neighbor search (IVF, PQ, etc.) - High performance on high-dimensional vectors - Optimized for large-scale datasets
Milvus	Zilliz	Open-source, cloud-native, and distributed	- Supports multiple ANN indexing methods (IVF, HNSW, PQ) - Handles both structured and unstructured data - Scalable architecture for massive feature vectors
Pinecone	Pinecone	Managed service; serverless vector search	- Automatic indexing and scaling - Real-time vector search with metadata filtering - Simplifies deployment and maintenance for production use
Vector Database	**Developer/ Organization**	**Deployment Model**	**Key Features**
Azure AI Search	Microsoft	Managed enterprise-grade solution integrated with Azure	- Hybrid search combining keyword and vector search - Uses ANN algorithms (e.g., HNSW) for efficient similarity matching - Integrated with Azure's ecosystem, offering strong security and compliance features

This table provides a high-level overview to help you determine the best choice based on your technical requirements, data scale, and operational preferences. Each option brings unique strengths, from FAISS's performance and scalability to Azure AI Search's seamless enterprise integration.

Conclusion

Vector databases are crucial for applications that require intuitive and adaptive responses, such as advanced search, personalization, and generative tasks. They provide flexibility to store and process complex, high-dimensional data, enabling technologies to "understand" relationships between data points. This, in turn, allows AI-driven systems to make more accurate recommendations, generate human-like responses, and handle intricate tasks with greater efficiency.

Exercise: Test Your Understanding

Answer the following questions and test your understanding of learning from

Chapter 3:

Q. 1. How do vector databases challenge the traditional notion of data storage, and what implications does this have for future AI applications?

Q. 2. Explain the difference between dot product, cosine similarity, and Euclidean distance as similarity measures used in vector databases?

Q. 3. What are vector embeddings?

Q. 4. What are some practical applications of vector databases in AI, and how do they enhance these applications.

Q. 5. Explain how different vector indexing techniques, such as KD-Trees, Ball Trees, LSH, and HNSW, contribute to the efficiency of vector databases.

Treat Prompts Like Conversations

The better you communicate with an AI model, the better it performs. Clear, structured prompts yield clearer, more useful results.

4

Retrieval-Augmented Generation

Creating relevant, accurate, and timely answers has become a big challenge for AI systems in the world of information. Traditional AI models, even those as advanced as large language models, struggle with one major limitation—**their training data is static**. Once a model is trained, it has no direct access to new or evolving data. Once these models are trained, they become like well-prepared students who studied hard for a competitive exam and dedicated countless hours to mastering history, memorizing every significant event, date, and figure from the past. This student excels at recounting the historical narratives of the world but neglects to stay updated on current affairs or recent developments. When exam day arrives, the student feels confident walking into the room, only to find that the exam questions cover various topics, including critical recent news events and emerging global issues. This scenario mirrors the limitations faced by AI models. While they can generate precise and coherent responses based on their training, they may falter when required to address newer, evolving topics not part of their training data.

The Problem with Static AI Models

This static nature leads to a common problem: the AI can produce articulate language but cannot often base its answers on the right, current facts. To illustrate this further Imagine you are on a long drive, and your car's navigation system confidently suggests a shortcut through a charming village, claiming it will save you two hours. Eager to reach your destination sooner, you take the route, only to find yourself on a narrow, winding road that suddenly ends due to construction work. Instead of the anticipated time savings, you end up stuck in traffic, watching your journey stretch far longer than expected because the navigation system lacked current information about the road conditions. This experience is like how large language models (LLMs) operate. Like the navigation system that confidently directs you through an unreliable path, LLMs can generate answers that sound authentic and assured but are often based on outdated or incomplete data. Like the navigation tool, LLMs work off a fixed dataset and cannot access real-time information about changes or developments worldwide. Let us look at another example. Law firms increasingly rely on AI to summarize case law, draft contracts, or provide legal insights. A firm is handling a complex contract dispute, and the AI assistant is tasked with analyzing previous similar cases. The problem? The AI's training data only includes legal decisions up until last year. However, this year's landmark ruling has dramatically changed the legal landscape for such disputes. The AI generates a summary based on outdated case law, leading the legal team down an incorrect path. If this erroneous information is missing, the firm could present a flawed argument, risking its reputation and losing the case.

This scenario mirrors a problem many organizations face when relying solely on AI systems that generate text based on static training data. Without real-time access to the latest legal decisions or external databases, the AI's responses are inherently limited, missing crucial developments that could impact the outcome. Another example is a healthcare provider utilizing an AI-powered diagnostic tool to assist in patient care. A doctor inputs symptoms a patient describes—persistent fatigue, joint pain, and skin rashes. The AI analyses the symptoms and generates a comprehensive report suggesting possible diagnoses, treatment options, and relevant studies. The report is polished and presents itself with an authoritative tone, with references to peer-reviewed articles. However, what the AI fails to incorporate is recent clinical research indicating that those specific symptoms can also be a result of a newly identified autoimmune disorder that emerged only weeks before. Instead, the AI relies on outdated medical guidelines that suggest more common conditions like rheumatoid arthritis or chronic fatigue syndrome. As a result, the doctor, confident in the AI's output, recommends a treatment plan based on the AI's suggestions. Unfortunately, this leads to a misdiagnosis and a delay in the patient receiving the correct treatment. The polished content of the AI's report creates a false sense of security, masking the underlying issue of missing crucial, real-time medical developments.

Bridging the Gap: Retrieval-Augmented Generation (RAG)

The question, then, is how to ensure that AI systems generate language well and do so with the most relevant and up-to-date data. The answer lies in bridging the gap between general-purpose language models and specialized, real-time data. This is where more advanced retrieval mechanisms come into play—ones that allow AI to reach beyond its pre-trained knowledge and tap into external sources, dynamically pulling in the data necessary to inform its responses.

As we navigate the complexities of ensuring that AI-generated outputs remain relevant and accurate, a solution emerges: Retrieval-Augmented Generation, commonly called RAG. This innovative technique bridges the gap between static knowledge and dynamic, real-time information, enhancing the AI's capability to produce context-aware responses.

RAG operates on a straightforward yet powerful premise: rather than solely relying on pre-existing training data; it incorporates relevant information from external sources into the generation process. Instead of merely regurgitating information learned during training, the AI can actively pull fresh data from databases, web content, or structured repositories to inform its outputs. The result? A more informed, accurate, and contextually relevant response that can significantly improve decision-making across various sectors.

Breaking Down RAG: A Well-Choreographed Trio

Think of Retrieval-Augmented Generation (RAG) as a highly coordinated relay race. Each team member has a specific role, ensuring the baton (information) moves smoothly from start to finish. The team consists of three key players: the Retriever, the Augmenter, and the Generator. Let us unpack their roles and how they work together to deliver accurate, context-rich responses.

Retriever: The Scout on the Team

Imagine the Retriever as a skilled scout venturing into a vast library of knowledge. It's a job? To quickly locate the most relevant books, chapters, or pages that hold the answer to your query. Instead of overwhelming the system with irrelevant data, the Retriever sharpens the focus, fetching only what is needed. For example, if the query is about renewable energy tax credits, the Retriever ensures it pulls out recent policy details instead of generic sustainability articles.

Augmenter: The Editor in Action

Now that the scout has returned the information, it is the Augmenter's turn to shine. Think of this as the editor who organizes the notes, highlights key points, and discards anything out of context. The Augmenter ensures the data aligns perfectly with the query, preparing it for the next step. It is like giving the Generator a neatly summarized cheat instead of an unorganized pile of documents.

Generator: The Storyteller Who Brings It All Together

Finally, the generator steps in as the storyteller. Armed with the input query and the augmented data, it crafts a coherent and insightful response. This is where the magic happens—combining raw information with contextual understanding to produce meaningful output. For instance, using the curated details on renewable energy tax credits, the Generator might draft an explanation tailored for a policy researcher, a small business owner, or an eco-conscious consumer.

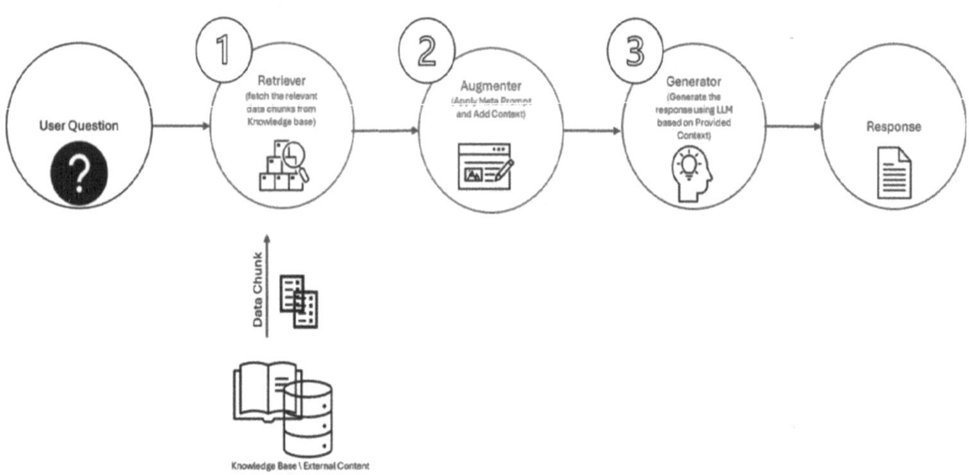

Fig 4.1: Diagram of a Retrieval-Augmented Generation (RAG) System Workflow

This diagram illustrates the workflow of a Retrieval-Augmented Generation (RAG) system, emphasizing the coordinated roles of the Retriever, Augmenter, and Generator in delivering accurate, context-rich responses.

Below is an explanation of each step:

- **User Question**: The process begins with a user submitting a question. This is represented by the circle with a question mark.
- **Retriever**: The first stage involves the Retriever, who acts as a skilled scout. The Retriever ventures into a vast library of knowledge (knowledge base or external content sources) to locate the most relevant data or chunks of information that hold the answer to the query. For example, if the query is about renewable energy tax credits, the Retriever ensures it pulls recent policy details instead of generic sustainability articles.
- **Augmenter**: In the second stage, the Augmenter takes the retrieved data and acts as an editor. The Augmenter organizes the notes, highlights key points, and discards anything out of context, ensuring the data aligns perfectly with the query. This is akin to providing the Generator with a neatly summarized cheat sheet

rather than an unorganized pile of documents.

- **Generator**: The third stage involves the Generator, who is the storyteller. Armed with the input query and the augmented data, the Generator crafts a coherent and insightful response. For instance, using the curated details on renewable energy tax credits, the Generator might draft an explanation tailored for a policy researcher, a small business owner, or an eco-conscious consumer.
- **Response**: The generated response is delivered to the user, completing the question-answering process.

Deep Dive into Retriever in RAG

In the **Retriever** is the gateway to the external knowledge base, ensuring that relevant and contextually appropriate information is delivered to the language model. Its effectiveness hinges on the type of database underpinning it, leading to two powerful variations: **Vector RAG** and **Graph RAG**.

Vector RAG: The Power of Vector Databases

A vector database operates on the principle of **embedding spaces**. Text, images, or other forms of data are converted into numerical representations called embeddings. These embeddings capture semantic meanings—essentially, similar concepts are represented as nearby points in the embedding space.

How It Works:

- When a query is submitted, it is transformed into an embedding using the exact mechanism.
- The Retriever searches the embedding space to find data points (e.g., documents or snippets) closest to the query regarding semantic similarity.
- These results are passed to the Augmenter for further processing.

Where Vector RAG Shines

Scenario: You are reviewing a contract with a renewable energy vendor and must ensure its clauses align with prior agreements.

- Using Vector RAG, you can retrieve similar clauses from previous contracts:
  - "Termination shall require a 90-day notice period."

    - "Breach of environmental compliance will result in contract nullification."

- This insight enables you to benchmark the current terms against past practices, ensuring consistency and minimizing risks.

But… What About Context?

While Vector RAG is fantastic at identifying semantically similar clauses, it has a **blind spot**: **contextual relationships.**

Here is the Challenge

Contracts are more than a collection of individual clauses—they are interconnected ecosystems.

For example:

- A **liability clause** might seem fine, but its **impact** could depend on the contract's penalty terms or delivery conditions.
- **Vector RAG** might return clauses that are similar in isolation but overlook their broader implications.

Real-World Limitation

You are assessing a clause about "on-time delivery penalties." Vector RAG can retrieve clauses with similar wording, but it might miss how this clause relates to:

- A vendor's historical performance (e.g., how often they have triggered penalties).
- Trends across multiple contracts with similar terms.

In this sense, Vector RAG offers a **microscope** for semantic detail but lacks the **map** to show the broader terrain.

Enter Graph RAG: The Missing Map

This is where **Graph RAG** fills the gaps left by Vector RAG. Unlike Vector RAG, which excels at finding individual puzzle pieces, Graph RAG is designed to understand **relationships** between those pieces.

How Graph RAG Complements Vector RAG

Where Vector RAG identifies similar clauses, Graph RAG reveals:

- How those clauses influence other parts of the contract.
- The historical context of a vendor's performance.
- Patterns of risk across related contracts.

Example: Contract Risk Assessment
Consider a complex scenario where you are evaluating risk within a renewable energy contract, mainly focusing on a liability clause related to force majeure events. The clause outlines conditions where vendors are excused from penalties due to unforeseen circumstances like natural disasters or regulatory changes. Here is how Graph RAG provides deeper, actionable insights:

- **Historical Connections**: The system connects this clause and similar clauses in past contracts. For example, it links your current liability clause to past contracts with similar vendors (such as Vendor X), showing how often similar clauses have been invoked and under what circumstances.
    - **Past Contracts**: Graph RAG might identify that in five previous contracts with Vendor X, the same force majeure clause was used, but disputes arose due to its vague language around "unforeseen events.

The Takeaway

With Vector RAG, you find the needle in the haystack. Graph RAG lets you understand how that needle fits into the larger fabric.

Let us investigate details when to use what:

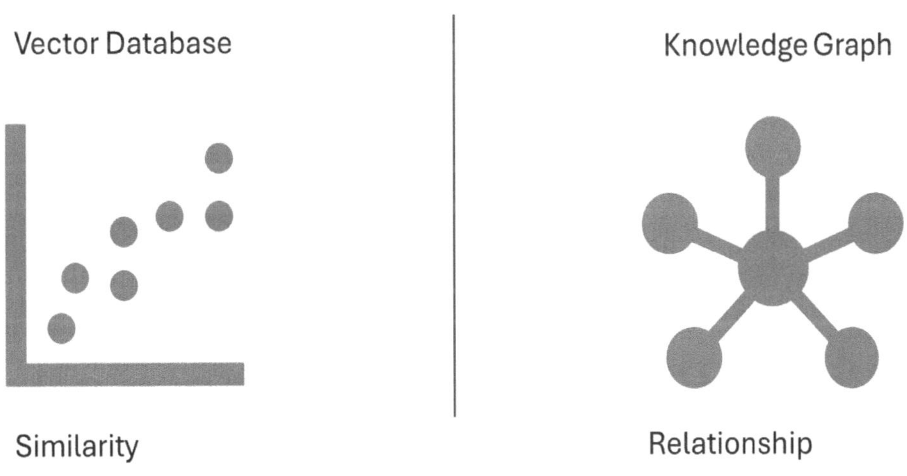

Fig 4.2: Comparison of Vector Database and Knowledge Graph

This figure illustrates the differences between Vector Database and Knowledge Graph in terms of similarity and relationship, respectively, showcasing how each approach addresses different data management and retrieval aspects. A Vector Database, illustrated on the left side of the image, utilizes vector space models to store and retrieve data based on similarity. Embedding data points into a high-dimensional space enables effective similarity search, making it useful for applications like recommendation systems where identifying similar items to a given query is essential. On the other hand, a Knowledge Graph, shown on the right, emphasizes the relationships between different data entities. It structures information in a graph format with nodes representing entities and edges denoting relationships, facilitating complex queries and data reasoning. This approach is beneficial for understanding interconnections, such as mapping relationships between authors and their co-authored publications.

Vector RAG vs. Graph RAG: Which to Use and When?

FEATURE	VECTOR RAG	GRAPH RAG
DATA STRUCTURE	Works with unstructured data (e.g., text).	Relies on structured, interconnected data.
BEST FOR	Semantic searches and context-aware retrieval.	Complex queries involving relationships between entities.
EXAMPLES	Clause searches, FAQ retrieval.	Risk assessment, vendor tracking, compliance mapping.
DATABASE	Vector database (e.g., Pinecone, Milvus, Azure AI Search).	Graph database (e.g., Neo4j, Cosmos DB).

Table 4.1: Comparison of vector RAG vs Graph RAG

As highlighted in Table 4.1, While **Vector RAG** is your go-to for semantic accuracy and speed, its strength lies in **isolated retrieval.** Graph RAG is the perfect complement for a complete picture that accounts for relationships and historical trends. Together, they form a **hybrid powerhouse—a hybrid RAG.**

Hybrid RAG: Combining Vector and Graph Power

Many real-world scenarios benefit from a **hybrid approach** that combines the strengths of Vector and Graph RAG.

Example Use Case: Compliance and Regulatory Insights

- **Scenario:** A procurement officer wants to ensure a vendor contract complies with both internal policies and environmental regulations.
- **Hybrid RAG Solution:**
    - **Vector RAG** retrieves semantically relevant clauses, like environmental compliance terms.

  - **Graph RAG** maps these clauses to legal frameworks (e.g., ISO standards, labor laws) stored as nodes in a knowledge graph.
  - Example insight: "Clause 4.3 aligns with ISO 14001 standards but lacks alignment with company policy on supplier sustainability reporting."
- **Benefit:** Ensures comprehensive compliance, reduces legal risks, and protects organizational reputation.

The Augmentation Engine: The Contextual Bridge

After the **Retriever** has gathered relevant data, the **Augmentation Engine** refines and enhances the raw information before passing it to the **Generator** (the core of the Large Language Model or LLM). Think of it as a chef preparing ingredients for a final dish—it is where the data is given context, organized, and augmented to create a more coherent and relevant prompt.

Role of the Augmentation Engine

The augmentation process is crucial because it ensures that the retrieved data integrates smoothly into the query, enhancing the LLM's ability to generate a focused, accurate response. Here is how the process works in more detail:

- **Combining Retrieved Data and User Query:** The augmentation engine combines the user's original query with the data fetched by the Retriever. This is akin to adding a few key ingredients to a base recipe — the augmentation engine ensures that the LLM will have the correct data and see it in the context of the user's original question.
- **Meta Prompts and Context Windows:** Meta prompts are specialized instructions that guide the LLM in processing the retrieved information. For example, if a user asks for "the key clauses in a vendor contract," the meta prompt might be something like, "Summarize the key clauses in the following text, making sure to highlight payment terms, risk clauses, and deadlines."
- Additionally, the augmentation engine manages **token limits** (the number of tokens or words that the LLM can process at once). This is crucial because LLMs have a context window limit. If the retrieved data exceeds this limit, the augmentation engine must decide which information is most important, ensuring the LLM works with a manageable, relevant subset.

The Generator: Creating Meaningful Responses

Once the **Augmentation Engine** has prepared the data and context, it is time for the **Generator**—the system's core powered by a large language model (LLM). This is where the real magic happens, as the LLM takes the augmented prompt (a combination of the user's query and relevant data) and generates a response.

Role of the Generator:

The Generator's job is to transform the structured prompt—enriched with retrieved information—into a coherent, contextually accurate response. This is where the true power of **Generative AI** comes into play, as the LLM uses its deep language understanding to provide a natural, human-like answer.

- **Contextual Awareness**: The LLM, already trained on vast amounts of data, now works with augmented data that is highly relevant to the user's query. The LLM's response becomes more grounded, accurate, and insightful by utilizing this specific, current information.
- **Response Creation**: The Generator does not just repeat facts; it synthesizes information from the augmented context to craft a narrative meaningfully answers the query. It goes beyond simple retrieval by interpreting, connecting, and summarizing the data.
- **User-Centric Focus**: The LLM also tailors the response to the user's needs. For instance, the response will be detailed and precise if the query is technical (e.g., related to a legal contract). If the query is more casual (e.g., asking about the general benefits of a product), the response will be concise and easier to understand.

Conclusion

This Chapter details the concept of Retrieval-Augmented Generation (RAG) as a solution to the limitations of static AI models, which cannot access new or evolving data post-training. RAG bridges this gap by integrating external, real-time information into AI-generated outputs, ensuring responses are both accurate and contextually relevant. The Chapter explains the RAG process through three key components: the Retriever, the Augmenter, and the Generator. Different approaches, Vector RAG and Graph RAG are compared for their strengths in semantic searches and context-aware retrieval versus understanding data relationships. A hybrid approach combining both methods, Hybrid RAG, is suggested for comprehensive solutions. The Augmentation Engine refines the Generator's data, producing meaningful, user-centric responses.

Exercise: Test Your Understanding

Answer the following questions and test your understanding of learning from `Chapter 4`:

`Q. 1.` How does RAG enhance the AI's ability to generate relevant responses?

`Q. 2.` What are the three key components of the RAG process?

`Q. 3.` What is the difference between Vector RAG and Graph RAG?

`Q. 4.` How does the Generator in the RAG framework create meaningful responses?

`Q. 5.` How does RAG address the issue of token limits in large language models (LLMs)?

Treat Prompts Like Conversations

The better you communicate with an AI model, the better it performs. Clear, structured prompts yield clearer, more useful results.

5

Fine-Tuning vs. RAG in Generative AI

In the previous chapter, we explored the power of Retrieval-Augmented Generation (RAG) and how it cleverly pairs large language models (LLMs) with external knowledge sources to generate accurate, context-rich responses. However, RAG, as versatile as it is, is not a one-size-fits-all solution. Some requirements go beyond what Retrieval alone can achieve, demanding deeper alignment between the AI system and a specific domain or task. When you rely solely on RAG, it is like having a high-performing but generalist assistant. It is quick, adaptable, and proficient in many areas. However, the moment you ask it to delve into the intricacies of your business—like evaluating a particular legal contract or generating a detailed response based on rare pharmaceutical research might falter. Why? Because generalist systems operate within the boundaries of their training and retrieval mechanisms, no matter how advanced.

Where RAG Shines—and Where It Stumbles

RAG excels in scenarios where accurate Retrieval is more important than deep specialization. For example:

- A procurement chatbot can use RAG to fetch supplier contract clauses quickly.
- A marketing assistant can retrieve past campaign performance reports to generate insights.
- A healthcare assistant can pull research papers related to a user's query about a particular disease.

However, let us consider more demanding scenarios:

- **Legal Analysis in Procurement**: Your system retrieves a supplier agreement clause mentioning "termination due to force majeure." The clause is relevant, but its applicability depends on the legal interpretation of the force majeure clause under specific regional laws—a nuance the system misses.

- **Healthcare Recommendations**: A patient-facing system retrieves general guidance for managing diabetes. However, tailoring advice for someone with specific conditions, such as Type 2 diabetes during pregnancy, requires not only retrieving the right content but also generating a response that aligns with the latest medical guidelines.
- **Financial Risk Assessment**: An investment assistant retrieves reports about market trends. However, assessing the impact of these trends on a niche market segment, like renewable energy in emerging economies, requires nuanced analysis.

In these cases, **Retrieval is not enough**. You need the system to deeply understand the context, make tailored inferences, and generate outputs that reflect domain expertise. This is where **fine-tuning** steps in. These scenarios underline the importance of **fine-tuning**—both for embedding generation and for the LLM itself.

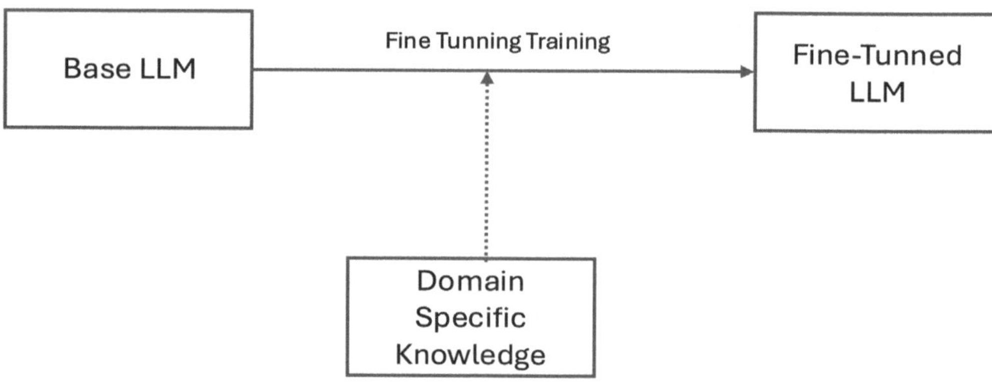

Fig. 5.1: Importance of Fine-Tuning in Enhancing AI Performance

The image illustrates fine-tuning a base Large Language Model (LLM) with domain-specific knowledge to create a fine-tuned LLM. This process goes beyond simple retrieval methods by integrating specialized information through fine-tuning training, enhancing the model's ability to generate contextually accurate and expert-level outputs.

Understanding Fine-Tuning: Two Dimensions

Fine-tuning comes in two Flavors, each addressing a specific gap in RAG:

- **Embedding Fine-Tuning** optimizes data retrieval by enhancing the vector representations of domain-specific concepts. For example, a generic embedding model might treat "cancer treatment" and "oncological therapy" in a pharmaceutical research database as loosely related. Fine-tuning can train the embeddings to treat these terms as interchangeable, improving the system's ability to surface the most relevant research papers.

- **Model Fine-Tuning**: Improving how responses are generated by aligning the language model with specific domain knowledge, style, or reasoning.

Delving into Fine-Tuning: How It Works and Why It Matters

Fine-tuning is customizing a pre-trained model to better suit a specific application, domain, or task. It leverages the foundational knowledge the model has already learned from its vast training data and refines it with domain-specific data. This approach improves precision and relevance, enabling AI to excel in niche areas where general-purpose models fall short.

How Fine-Tuning Works

Fine-tuning involves **training** a model on a carefully curated dataset to modify its behavior or output. Here is how the process unfolds for embeddings and GPT models:

Fine-Tuning Embeddings: Enhancing Retrieval
Embedding models convert text into numeric vectors that capture the meaning and relationships between words or phrases. Fine-tuning embeddings is like teaching the system a specialized language.

- **Step 1: Curate Domain-Specific Data:** Gather examples of domain-specific phrases, terms, and contexts. For instance, in a **legal domain**, you might include data showing how "liquidated damages" relate to "contract breach penalties."
- **Step 2: Train in Similarity Tasks:** The model is trained to recognize semantic relationships between terms. For example:
    - Input 1: “force majeure”
    - Input 2: “unforeseen circumstances clause”
    - Desired Output: High similarity score.

This process refines the embeddings, making them better at retrieving documents matching user queries' intent.

Example: Improved Search in Procurement
A procurement officer searching for "early termination fees" in contracts may retrieve results containing synonyms like "exit penalties" or "cancellation charges," even if those terms are not explicitly mentioned in the query. Fine-tuning embeddings ensure these relationships are captured, improving search precision.

Fine-Tuning LLM Models: Customizing Response Generation

Fine-tuning an LLM model is more comprehensive, as it adjusts how it generates responses based on new patterns and knowledge introduced during training.

- **Step 1: Gather Task-Specific Data:**Collect datasets relevant to your domain or use case. For instance:
    - In **healthcare**, use case reports and medical guidelines.
    - In **finance**, risk analysis reports and regulatory policies are used.
- **Step 2: Apply Supervised Fine-Tuning:** The model is exposed to input-output pairs, learning to replicate the desired behavior. For example:
    - Input: "What is the recommended dosage for a Type 2 diabetic?"
    - Output: "The recommended dosage of Metformin for adults with Type 2 diabetes is 500 mg twice daily, based on clinical guidelines."
- **Step 3: Evaluate and Adjust:** Fine-tuned models are tested for accuracy, tone, and consistency, ensuring they meet the domain's requirements.

Example: Tailored Customer Support

A fine-tuned GPT model for an **airline customer support bot** could handle nuanced queries like:

- **Generic Model Response**: "The layover policy depends on the airline's terms and conditions."
- **Fine-Tuned Model Response**: "For layovers exceeding 8 hours on international flights, you may qualify for free accommodation and meal vouchers as per our policy. Please check eligibility based on your ticket class."

When Fine-Tuning Makes a Difference

While general-purpose models work well for broad use cases, fine-tuning adds significant value in the following scenarios:

- **High Complexity and Precision Needs:** In fields like law, medicine, or engineering, incorrect or vague responses can lead to costly mistakes.
  Example: In a legal assistant, fine-tuning ensures that advice on "data protection laws" complies with GDPR and local regulations.
- **Domain-Specific Vocabulary:** Models pre-trained on general datasets may lack an understanding of niche terminologies.
  Example: A fine-tuned financial assistant understands terms like "carry trade,"

"hedging," and "sovereign risk."

- **Tone and Branding Consistency:** Fine-tuning helps models align responses with an organization's voice.
  Example: A luxury brand chatbot uses fine-tuning to ensure its responses are polite, elegant, and aspirational.
- **Multi-Turn Conversations:** Fine-tuned models excel at maintaining context over more extended dialogues.
  Example: A healthcare assistant can answer a patient's follow-up questions consistently and empathetically.

Challenges of Fine-Tuning

While fine-tuning adds immense value by tailoring AI systems to specific needs, it has hurdles. Businesses and developers must navigate challenges related to data preparation, resource allocation, and the potential trade-offs between specialization and generality.

Data Preparation: The Cornerstone of Fine-Tuning

Fine-tuning is only as good as the data you feed into it. The quality, quantity, and relevance of training data are critical. Let us break this down:

Challenge: Gathering High-Quality Data

Curating a domain-specific dataset requires significant effort. Consider a financial assistant tasked with analyzing investment risks. The data must include:

- Historical market trends.
- Case studies of past investment decisions.
- Risk assessment frameworks for various industries.

Example: You may need contract documents, supplier risk assessments, and compliance regulations for a procurement AI assistant. However, many organizations store such data in unstructured formats—scattered PDFs, emails, or spreadsheets—making it difficult to compile and clean.

Challenge: Data Annotation

Once you have the data, it must be labeled or annotated to provide clear examples for the model to learn from.

Example: In a legal assistant, clauses related to "intellectual property rights" might need tags like "ownership," "licensing," and "infringement penalties." Poorly labeled data can lead to a model that retrieves irrelevant information or generates incorrect outputs.

Resource Demands: Time, Compute, and Expertise

Fine-tuning requires significant computational resources, skilled personnel, and time. Let us break it down:

Compute Costs

Fine-tuning large models like GPT-3 involve high computational expenses. Training can take hours or days, even on advanced GPUs or TPUs.

Example: Fine-tuning GPT for a healthcare assistant using datasets of clinical guidelines and case studies might require dozens of hours on a multi-GPU system, driving up costs.

Expertise Gap

Fine-tuning is not plug-and-play. It demands expertise in:

- Understanding the model architecture.
- Crafting adequate training datasets.
- Evaluating fine-tuned models for accuracy, fairness, and ethical compliance.

Example: An organization might fine-tune a model for legal risk analysis but fail to account for bias in training data—such as focusing on U.S. legal systems while ignoring international laws. This could lead to incomplete or incorrect outputs for global users.

Balancing Generality and Specialization

Fine-tuned models often excel in a specific domain but may lose their general-purpose capabilities. This trade-off can limit the system's versatility.

Example: Overfitting in Niche Domains
A fine-tuned financial assistant might perform exceptionally well when analyzing bond markets but struggles with general queries about stock performance.

If the model is overfitted to a narrow dataset, it can become brittle and less adaptable to new or adjacent tasks.

Solution: Hybrid Approaches
Combining fine-tuning with RAG can help balance generality and specialization: Use RAG for general Retrieval and fine-tuning for domain-specific reasoning.

Example: A legal AI assistant retrieves clauses using RAG but generates nuanced legal opinions through a fine-tuned GPT model.

Maintaining Model Freshness

Fine-tuning a model locks it into the patterns and knowledge of its training data. Over time, this can lead to outdated or irrelevant outputs.

Example: A healthcare assistant fine-tuned 2022 clinical guidelines might not include newer treatment protocols introduced in 2024.

Solution: Periodic Updates
To ensure relevance:
- Periodically fine-tune the model with updated datasets.
- Incorporate external retrieval mechanisms (e.g., RAG) to pull the latest real-time data.

Ethical and Compliance Considerations

Fine-tuning introduces unique ethical challenges. Models trained on sensitive or biased data can perpetuate or amplify these biases.

Example: Bias in Legal AI
If fine-tuning relies on case law predominantly from jurisdictions favoring corporate interests, the model might generate responses that align disproportionately with corporate perspectives, neglecting individual rights.

Solution: Mitigating Bias
- Perform rigorous testing to identify and mitigate bias.

- Incorporate diverse datasets representing varied perspectives.

Best Practices for Fine-Tuning: Setting Up for Success

While powerful, fine-tuning requires careful planning and execution to achieve the desired results. Following best practices ensures that the process is efficient, the outcomes are reliable, and the system aligns with your objectives. This section focuses on key strategies for successful fine-tuning.

Define Clear Objectives

Before starting the fine-tuning process, defining what success looks like is essential.

Questions to Ask:

- What problem are we solving?
  For example, are we improving retrieval accuracy or making response generation more domain-specific?
- Who are the end users?
  Understanding the target audience—procurement professionals, healthcare providers, or legal advisors—guides the fine-tuning of the model.
- What is the expected output?
  Should the responses be concise, detailed, formal, or conversational?

Example: A procurement chatbot may need to provide a compliance report for contracts, whereas a legal assistant should give detailed risk analyses.

Prepare High-Quality Training Data

The data you use for fine-tuning directly affects the model's performance.

Key Strategies:

- Curate Relevant Data:
    - Gather domain-specific documents, such as contracts, case studies, or regulatory guidelines.
    - Avoid including irrelevant or outdated information.
- Balance Diversity and Specificity:
    - While focusing on your domain, include examples that cover a wide range of scenarios.

Example: For a legal assistant, balance training data with clauses related to intellectual property, confidentiality, and liability.

- Annotate Clearly:
    - Use human experts to tag the data with specific labels, ensuring the model learns from accurate examples.

Start with Lightweight Fine-Tuning

Fine-tuning does not always mean reworking the entire model. In many cases, you can focus on adjusting specific layers or components.

Approaches to Lightweight Fine-Tuning:

- **Adapter Layers**: Add small trainable layers to the pre-trained model while keeping the original weights intact. This reduces the computational cost and the risk of overfitting.
- **Parameter-Efficient Fine-Tuning**: Modify only a subset of the model's parameters, such as attention heads or embeddings.

  Example: For a supply chain assistant, lightweight fine-tuning on terminology like "Just-in-Time inventory" or "economic order quantity" ensures relevant Retrieval without requiring an overhaul of the entire model.

Evaluate Iteratively

Fine-tuning is an iterative process. Evaluating the model at each stage ensures that changes improve performance without unintended consequences.

Metrics to Track:

- **Precision and Recall**: How well does the model retrieve relevant information?
- **Response Quality**: Are the generated answers accurate, coherent, and aligned with the domain?
- **User Satisfaction**: Do test users find the outputs helpful and intuitive?

Example: For a fine-tuned contract review assistant:

- Test if it retrieves all relevant clauses for a query like "termination penalties."
- Check if the generated summaries are clear and legally sound.

Incorporate Human Feedback

Even the best-fine-tuned models benefit from human validation. Human-in-the-loop (HITL) workflows ensure the system evolves based on real-world usage.

Steps to Implement HITL:

- Deploy the fine-tuned model in a controlled environment (e.g., pilot phase).
- Gather user feedback on accuracy, usability, and gaps.
- Use this feedback to refine the training data or adjust model parameters.

Example: A fine-tuned medical assistant might initially struggle with nuanced patient queries. Feedback from doctors can highlight specific areas for improvement, such as drug interactions or rare diseases.

Integrate Safeguards for Bias and Ethics

Bias can creep into fine-tuned models, particularly when the training data reflects historical or systemic biases. Addressing this proactively is critical.

How to Mitigate Bias?

- **Diverse Training Data**: Ensure the dataset represents varied demographics, industries, or use cases.
- **Bias Testing**: Evaluate the model's outputs for fairness across different groups or scenarios.
- **Auditing and Documentation**: Keep detailed records of the fine-tuning process to ensure transparency.

Example: A fine-tuned financial assistant trained in Western market data might overemphasize strategies like hedge funds, neglecting the context of emerging markets. Including diverse datasets ensures balanced advice.

Monitor Post-Deployment Performance

Fine-tuning does not end with deployment. Continuous monitoring ensures that the model adapts to evolving needs and maintains relevance.

Key Activities

- **Track KPIs**: Measure how the model performs against predefined metrics over time.
- **Update Training Data**: Incorporate new information or address gaps identified during deployment.
- **Enable RAG Integration**: Combine the fine-tuned model with a retrieval mechanism for real-time updates.

Example: A fine-tuned legal AI assistant might initially excel in contract review but struggle to adapt when new regulations are introduced. Regular updates ensure its effectiveness.

The Synergy of RAG and Fine-Tuning: A Hybrid Approach

While Retrieval-Augmented Generation (RAG) and fine-tuning are powerful in isolation, their combination can create solutions that harness the best of both worlds. This hybrid approach addresses limitations in retrieval accuracy, contextual relevance, and response customization, making it ideal for complex, dynamic applications.

Think of RAG and fine-tuning as a chef and a recipe:

- **RAG (Chef)**: Fetches a pantry's best ingredients (data).
- **Fine-Tuned GPT (Recipe)**: Transforms those ingredients into a gourmet meal (meaningful responses).

Without the chef, you would struggle to find the right ingredients. Without the recipe, the meal would lack flavor or structure. Together, they create something exceptional.

Handling Long-Tail Queries with Hybrid RAG and Fine-Tuning

One challenge in AI systems is addressing *long-tail queries*, which are rare or complex user questions that are difficult to predict during model training.

How the Hybrid Approach Helps?

- RAG pulls relevant documents from a vast corpus, ensuring coverage for obscure topics.
- Fine-tuned GPT adapts the retrieved content into meaningful, context-aware responses.

Example: In a legal scenario, a user might ask:

- Query: What precedents support tenant rights in co-tenancy disputes?
- Hybrid Workflow:
    - RAG retrieves case laws, articles, and statutory clauses related to co-tenancy.

- Fine-tuned GPT synthesizes this information into a concise response:
- "The landmark case Rajesh vs. Sumit (2024) established that co-tenants have equal rights to shared property unless otherwise specified in the lease agreement."

By merging the precision of RAG with the domain-specific adaptability of fine-tuning, you create a robust, scalable AI solution capable of addressing a broad spectrum of queries. The following section will explore evaluation metrics and deployment strategies for hybrid systems to ensure optimal performance.

Conclusion

The current chapter comprehensively analyzes Retrieval-Augmented Generation (RAG) and fine-tuning approaches to enhancing AI performance. While RAG excels in retrieving accurate, context-rich information from external sources, it often falters with complex, domain-specific queries requiring deep understanding, such as legal analysis or personalized healthcare recommendations. Fine-tuning addresses these limitations by customizing pre-trained models with domain-specific knowledge, improving precision and relevance. However, fine-tuning requires high-quality training data and significant computational resources. Combining RAG and fine-tuning in a hybrid approach leverages the strengths of both methods, offering versatile solutions that handle a broad spectrum of queries while maintaining specialized expertise. This strategic application ensures AI models are adaptable and deeply knowledgeable, effectively meeting diverse user needs.

Exercise: Test Your Understanding

Answer the following questions and test your understanding of learning from **Chapter 5**:

Q. 1. What are the primary limitations of Retrieval-Augmented Generation (RAG)?

Q. 2. How does fine-tuning enhance AI performance compared to RAG?

Q. 3. What are the key challenges associated with fine-tuning AI models?

Q. 4. How does a hybrid approach combining RAG and fine-tuning improve AI solutions?

Q. 5. Why is it essential to integrate safeguards for bias and ethics in fine-tuning?

6

Introduction to Prompt Engineering

Have you ever tried explaining a task to someone, only to realize they did the opposite of what you intended? The same principle applies to Generative AI. To get the results you want, you must communicate concisely and precisely—and this is where **prompt engineering** becomes crucial. Imagine walking into a grand exhibition hall tasked with curating an unforgettable visitor experience. You have been given the theme: **Dinosaurs**. What an exciting challenge! However, without a clear plan, the possibilities are overwhelming. Should the focus be on their towering skeletons, the intricate science of their extinction, or immersive recreation of their ancient habitats? A simple directive like *"Set up a dinosaur exhibit"* leaves too much room for interpretation and risks delivering something underwhelming—like a few dusty fossils on pedestals. Now, picture this instead: You are designing the exhibit for children aged 8–12 to spark their curiosity and make learning fun. You envision a **life-sized T-Rex roaring to greet visitors**, interactive displays that let kids "feed" virtual herbivores and carnivores, and a sandbox where they can uncover replicas of ancient fossils like junior paleontologists. The goal is clear: immerse these young learners in the world of dinosaurs, blending education with entertainment.

This detailed vision does not just inform—it inspires your team, setting the stage for an experience that will leave a lasting impact. Every exhibit piece is aligned with your purpose, from the lighting that dramatizes the T-Rex's sharp teeth to the playful quizzes explaining why herbivores preferred plants over protein. Crafting prompts for AI is much like curating that dinosaur exhibit. A vague instruction like *"Describe dinosaurs"* is like saying, *"Create an exhibit."* The result may be technically correct but lacks the depth or relevance to engage genuinely. However, when you craft a prompt with precision, context, and intent, AI becomes your collaborator in creating something extraordinary. Think of prompt engineering as drafting the perfect instructions for a hyper-intelligent assistant. If you tell it precisely what you need, it can help you craft reports, generate code, write stories, and much more.

However, the result might be off-track or even irrelevant if you are vague or unclear. This is where **Prompt Engineering** comes into play. It is the art and science of crafting questions and commands that yield the best possible outcomes from a Generative AI.

This chapter will delve into prompt engineering's core, exploring what it is, why it is critical, and how to master it to transform your interaction with AI.

Understanding a Prompt

A **prompt** is an input you provide to a Generative AI model, like OpenAI's GPT series, to guide its response. It can be a question, an instruction, or even a snippet of text to complete. Prompts set the AI's output's context, tone, and boundaries.

For example, consider these two prompts:

- "Explain climate change."
- "Explain climate change to a 10-year-old using simple examples."

The first Prompt is open-ended and may result in a technical explanation. The second is more specific, setting a target audience (a 10-year-old) and a desired tone (example-driven and straightforward). The difference in specificity leads to vastly different outputs.

Generative AI models like GPT are compelling but only as good as the instructions they receive.

Poorly designed prompts can lead to:

- Vague or irrelevant responses
- Misinterpretation of context
- Missed opportunities to leverage the model's full potential

However, with **thoughtful prompts**, you can unlock:

- **Precision**: Get the exact information or creative output you need.
- **Efficiency**: Save time by minimizing back-and-forth refinements.
- **Insightfulness**: Generate responses that go beyond surface-level answers.

Key Principals for Crafting Prompts

Effective prompts share common traits that make them successful. Adhering to these guidelines will significantly enhance the quality of AI-generated responses.

Be Specific, Not Vague

- Instead of: "Explain machine learning."
- Try: "Explain the concept of supervised learning in machine learning with an example involving image classification."

- The more precise you are, the more targeted the output will be.

Use Examples to Clarify Intent

- AI models often work better when they have examples to reference. For instance, if you are generating product descriptions, you might add:
- "Here is an example of a product description for a coffee maker: 'Brew your perfect cup of coffee every time with this sleek, modern coffee maker designed to preserve the rich flavor of your beans.'"

Set Expectations

- Do not just ask the AI to generate text—tell it what you want the text to do.
- Instead of: "Write a blog post about AI."
- Try: "Write a blog post of 500 words explaining how AI is transforming the healthcare industry, with a focus on patient care improvements."

Incorporate Constraints

- Constraints help the AI narrow down the scope of its response. These might include word limits, tone, or even structure.
  For example: "Generate a tweet about the benefits of AI in business, using no more than 140 characters and maintaining a friendly, casual tone."

Leverage Role-Specific Prompts

To improve the relevance of the AI's response, consider framing your prompts with the perspective of a specific role or stakeholder. By identifying the role, the AI should adopt—whether a lawyer, a marketing expert, or a financial analyst—you can ensure that the response aligns more closely with that role's knowledge and priorities.

Example: Consider following prompt:
Generic Prompt: "Write a business proposal."
Role-Specific Prompt: "Write a business proposal for a new software product tailored for senior executives in the healthcare industry, focusing on cost savings and improved patient outcomes."

This helps the AI narrow its focus and align its output with the expectations and requirements of a specific audience.

Mind Length and Complexity

While it is important to be specific and detailed, you also want to ensure that your prompts remain concise and manageable. Lengthy and overly complex prompts can confuse the AI and lead to unclear or convoluted responses. Try to balance specificity with brevity. If your Prompt is too long, consider breaking it into smaller, more manageable chunks.

Consider following example:

- Overly Complex Prompt: "Given the detailed market trends of the past five years, the current political and economic climate, and the shifts in consumer behavior in the digital age, summarize the potential impact on the luxury goods sector over the next decade, including expected growth rates, key market drivers, and the role of technology in shaping demand."
- Refined Prompt: "Summarize the market outlook for the luxury goods sector over the next decade, highlighting key drivers like technology, consumer behavior, and economic factors." By simplifying Prompt, the AI will have a more explicit focus and be more likely to produce a concise and relevant response.

Iterate and Refine

Sometimes, the first response will not be exactly what you need. Do not hesitate to refine your Prompt based on the output you receive. You can always go back and add more context or change the phrasing to get better results.

Anticipating Questions and Misconceptions

One common question is: "*Why can't the AI figure this out?*" The answer lies in how AI operates. Generative models do not think or infer like humans; they process patterns in data. Without guidance, their output reflects the ambiguity of the input. A vague prompt is like handing a map without a destination—it might get you somewhere, but not where you want to go. Another misconception is: *"More detail always means better prompts."* While detail helps, too much irrelevant information can confuse the model. The key is **relevance**. Provide only the details that serve the goal, like specifying the audience, purpose, and outcome.

Why This Matters

Imagine the potential impact of mastering this skill. From drafting compelling marketing copy to designing intricate workflows, prompt engineering transforms AI from a tool into a creative and strategic partner. It saves time, enhances output quality, and empowers you to tackle complex challenges precisely. So, the next time you interact with AI, think of yourself as a curator shaping an experience, telling a story, and delivering value. A well-crafted prompt is your blueprint for success—building an exhibit, writing an article, or unlocking the limitless potential of generative AI.

Prompt Chaining and Modular Prompts

Once you have mastered crafting precise and purposeful prompts, the question becomes: *"How do I scale this for more complex, multi-layered tasks?"* Imagine moving from creating a single exhibit room to designing an entire museum. Each room must align with the overarching theme yet offers a unique story. In AI, scaling prompt engineering involves chaining instructions, orchestrating multiple outputs, and embedding iterative refinement. Let us return to our dinosaur analogy. Suppose your museum now includes zones for paleontology, climate science, and extinction theories. To create a cohesive visitor journey, you would design each zone with distinct content but ensure a unified narrative arc. Similarly, when tackling intricate AI tasks—such as generating a comprehensive business proposal, analyzing legal documents, or drafting a multi-part report—you need to think of prompts as interconnected components working toward a shared goal.

Breaking Down Complex Tasks

Consider a real-world example: drafting a **contract risk assessment** using AI. This is not a one-prompt task; it involves multiple stages:

- Extracting Key Clauses: Identify critical sections such as payment terms, confidentiality, indemnity, and liability.
    - Prompt Example: "From this contract, extract all confidentiality, liability, and indemnity clauses and summarize each in one sentence. Highlight any sections with ambiguous or missing details."
- Assessing Risks: Evaluate potential red flags in the extracted clauses.
    - Prompt Example: "Based on the summarized clauses, identify risks using the following categories: financial, operational, and reputational. Provide a 2–3 sentence explanation for each flagged risk."
- Recommending Mitigations: Offer actionable steps to address identified risks.
    - Prompt Example: "For each identified risk, suggest specific mitigation strategies. Use concise, actionable language suitable for a legal advisory document."
- Compiling the Report: Combine the outputs into a structured, professional report.
    - Prompt Example: "Draft a report summarizing the identified key clauses, risks, and mitigation strategies. Use the following structure: (1) Executive Summary, (2) Key Clauses, (3) Risk Assessment, (4) Recommendations. Write in a formal tone."

This modular approach allows you to tackle one puzzle piece at a time, ensuring precision and clarity at each step while maintaining alignment with the larger objective.

Instructing Models to Handle Unknowns

What happens when the AI encounters conflicting or insufficient information? You can explicitly instruct it to acknowledge uncertainty rather than forcing a guess.

For example:

"If the information is unclear or contradictory, respond with: 'The available data does not provide a definitive answer. Based on the information provided, here are the possible explanations...'"

This approach improves the reliability of the AI's responses and builds trust by transparently communicating limitations.

Evaluating and Optimizing Prompt Effectiveness

Crafting and refining our prompts is key to success when working with Generative AI. However, even the most well-constructed Prompt is not always perfect on the first try. That is where the art of evaluation and optimization comes into play—two essential components of prompt engineering that allow you to continually improve your AI interactions and ensure consistently high-quality results. Imagine you are a chef whose goal is to create the perfect dish. The ingredients represent your prompts; the final meal is the AI's output. No matter how skilled you are in the kitchen, you might need to adjust the seasoning, tweak the cooking time, or swap an ingredient to get the flavor right. Similarly, practical prompt engineering involves evaluating the results, understanding how the AI responds, and adjusting improve your outcomes over time.

Metrics for Success: How to Measure Prompt Quality

Establishing clear metrics is the first step in evaluating the effectiveness of your prompts. You would not serve a dish without tasting it first, and you should not accept AI outputs without considering their quality.

So, what makes "good" prompt? Here are the key metrics to focus on:

- **Relevance**: Does the AI's response align with your expectations or the task? For instance, if you use an AI to generate a report, does the output provide relevant insights that meet the report's requirements? If your Prompt concerns a contract review, does the AI focus on the key clauses, or does it miss important details?
- **Accuracy**: Is the information the AI provides factual and precise? Accuracy is crucial when using AI for legal research, technical troubleshooting, or customer support, where even minor errors can lead to significant consequences.
- **Coherence**: Does the response make sense and flow logically? A coherent AI output is easy to read and understand. If the AI produces disjointed or

contradictory statements, it is a sign that the Prompt may need to be refined.

- **Creativity**: Depending on your task, you may value creativity. For instance, when using an AI for content generation (e.g., writing blog posts, generating marketing copy), how original and engaging is the response? An excellent creative output should surprise you positively while still being aligned with the Prompt's goal.

Using these metrics, you can assess whether your Prompt generates the desired outcomes. Remember that a successful prompt may excel in some areas while needing improvement in others. For example, an AI-generated marketing slogan might be highly creative but lack clarity or relevance to your brand's tone. This is where the optimization process comes in.

Feedback Loops: Refining Prompts Based on Results

Evaluating the effectiveness of your prompts is only the first step—optimization is a continual journey. Once you have assessed the quality of the AI's output, the next step is to refine your prompts based on the feedback you receive from the AI's responses. Here is where the analogy of a feedback loop comes in: just as a musician adjusts their performance after each playthrough, refining their technique with each rendition, you, too, can adjust and improve your prompts with each iteration. For instance, imagine you are working on an AI prompt to generate customer support responses. The first time you run Prompt, the AI might respond excellently to simple queries but struggle with more complex ones. By carefully analyzing its shortcomings, perhaps the AI does not understand the tone you want or provides overly generic answers—you can tweak the Prompt for better results.

This might involve:

- **Adding more context**: If the AI is not responding as expected, you may need to provide additional context. For example, instead of asking, "What are the benefits of your product?" you could specify, "What are the top three benefits of your product for a small business owner interested in saving time and reducing costs?"
- **Rephrasing the Prompt**: Sometimes, small changes in phrasing can drastically change the AI's response. Instead of a broad question like "Tell me about marketing strategies," try focusing on a more specific aspect like "What are the top five digital marketing strategies for a B2B SaaS company in 2024?"
- **Including examples**: Showing the AI an example of the response you expect can be a game-changer. This will guide the model and help it understand the tone, format, and structure you aim for.

This iterative evaluation and refinement process ensures that your prompts evolve to meet the specific needs of your use case, enhancing the AI's performance over time.

Leveraging User Data to Enhance Prompts

In many cases, the true power of prompt optimization lies in leveraging real-world data—particularly user feedback and behavior. Let us take a scenario where you build an AI-powered tool for a customer service department. Initially, your prompts may generate generic responses. However, you can adjust your prompts to provide more targeted and practical solutions as you gather more user data—such as common queries, customer sentiment, or frequently asked questions. For instance, if users frequently ask about the same issue, you can design a prompt that anticipates this need, ensuring that the AI's response is more relevant and immediate. Additionally, tracking user engagement with AI-generated responses can provide insights into how well the prompts work. If users engage more with certain types of responses, this signals that the prompt structure is adequate. Conversely, low engagement could indicate that the prompt needs refinement. You can optimize your prompts by continuously iterating based on user data to ensure they consistently generate the best possible outputs. This approach also helps tailor the AI's responses to the unique needs of your audience or business.

Addressing Ambiguity and Ensuring Consistency

A common challenge in prompt engineering is dealing with ambiguity. Ambiguous prompts lead to varied AI responses, making predicting or relying on the output difficult. By focusing on clarity and eliminating uncertainty from your prompts, you ensure the AI understands precisely what you are asking for. This might mean specifying terms the AI might interpret differently or breaking down complex questions into simpler parts. Inconsistencies can arise when prompts are vague or leave room for multiple interpretations. Consistent, prompt engineering is key to ensuring that the AI behaves predictably, regardless of the complexity of the task at hand.

Key Prompt Engineering Techniques

In this section, we will explore some of the key techniques-

- **Zero-shot Prompting** requires no prior examples or training and relies on the LLM's pre-trained knowledge. It is ideal for simple queries or tasks where the model can infer answers directly.
  Example in Manufacturing: A plant manager wants to monitor energy efficiency:
  Prompt: "Identify the three most energy-intensive processes in this week's production data and suggest improvements."

  Output

  - Plastic molding: Reduce reheating cycles.

  - Metal forging: Optimize furnace temperatures.
  - Welding: Switch to energy-efficient equipment.

This straightforward approach saves time for decision-makers by quickly surfacing insights without additional context.

- **Few-shot Prompting** provides the LLM with examples to guide its response. This technique is helpful for tasks requiring nuance or contextual understanding.

  Example in Retail: A retail chain needs to classify customer feedback into actionable categories:
  Prompt: "Classify feedback as follows:
    - 'Great sound quality but bulky design.' → [Category: Design Issue]
    - 'Fast delivery but high shipping cost.' → [Category: Shipping Concern]

  Now classify these:
    - 'Excellent quality but poor packaging.'
    - 'Affordable pricing but slow delivery.'"

  Output:
    - [Category: Packaging Concern]
    - [Category: Shipping Concern]

  Few-shot prompting provides SMEs with granular insights tailored to their use cases.

- **Chain-of-Thought (CoT) Prompting** the Chain of Thought (CoT) technique guides a model through a structured step-by-step reasoning process to solve complex problems. It breaks down the problem into smaller parts, ensuring logical clarity and accuracy, especially for tasks requiring multi-step reasoning.

  Key Elements
    - Step-by-Step Reasoning: The model addresses each part of the problem sequentially.
    - Intermediate Calculations: The model makes intermediate inferences or calculations.
    - Explicit Logic: The reasoning process is shown transparently.
    - Iterative Process: Each step builds toward the final answer.

  Example in the Mobility Sector
  Problem: Which delivery option is faster?
    - Option 1: Drive a truck 100 miles at 50 mph.
    - Option 2: Drive a van 60 miles at 40 mph, then ride a motorcycle 40 miles at 60 mph.

Step 1: Calculate the time for each option.
For Option 1:
Time = Distance ÷ Speed = 100 miles ÷ 50 mph = 2 hours.
For Option 2:
Time for van = 60 miles ÷ 40 mph = 1.5 hours.
Time for motorcycle = 40 miles ÷ 60 mph = 0.67 hours.
Total time for Option 2 = 1.5 + 0.67 = 2.17 hours.

Step 2: Compare the results.
Option 1 takes 2 hours, while Option 2 takes 2.17 hours.
Conclusion: Option 1 is faster, taking less time than Option 2.

Benefits of Chain of Thought:

- Improved Accuracy: Breaks down the problem, reducing mistakes.
- Transparency: Intermediate steps make reasoning more apparent.
- Error Reduction: Ensures no steps are skipped, leading to correct results.

This technique helps solve complex, multi-step problems in mobility, logistics, and business decision-making.

- **Meta Prompting** involves using a high-level prompt to guide a language model (LM) in breaking down complex tasks into smaller sub-tasks, delegating these to specialized expert models, and coordinating their responses. Let us consider a detailed scenario where meta-prompting can significantly improve the insights you get from a production report.
  Simple Prompt

  "Summarize the weekly production data: {data}"

  The output here might be:

  "The factory produced 5,000 units, with some downtime noted."

  This is useful but lacks specificity. The challenge is making this summary more actionable by breaking the data into relevant insights, such as identifying bottlenecks or inefficiencies.

  The Meta-Prompt:
  Instead of just refining the Prompt, the meta-prompt introduces a high-level framework that instructs the LM to break down the task and engage specialized experts:

Improve the following Prompt:

- Breaking down the weekly production data into key components: machine performance, downtime analysis, and shift-based productivity.

- Assigning each component to an expert model:

- Expert 1: Analyse machine downtime, identify machines with the highest downtime, and suggest potential fixes.

- Expert 2: Analyse production efficiency, highlight inefficiencies, and suggest ways to streamline operations.

- Expert 3: Examine seasonal trends in production, considering the time of year and external factors that might influence output.

Ensure that the responses from each expert are logically connected and produce a comprehensive, actionable summary.

{simple_prompt}

The Output

The meta-prompt triggers the LM to perform its conductor role. It interacts with the expert models, ensuring they generate focused outputs like:

- **Expert 1**: "Machine A has experienced 15% more downtime than other machines, primarily due to recurring issues with its motor. Suggest scheduling more frequent maintenance."
- **Expert 2**: "There is a noticeable inefficiency in the afternoon shift, likely due to reduced worker productivity after lunch. Implementing shift optimization could improve efficiency by 10%."
- **Expert 3**: "During the summer months, production typically slows down by 5% due to temperature-related issues with the machinery. Adjusting the temperature control settings could mitigate this drop."

The LM then combines these insights, ensuring they align and present a coherent summary:

"This week, machine A experienced significant downtime due to recurring motor issues, which could be mitigated by more frequent maintenance. The afternoon shift is underperforming, with a 10% efficiency gap compared to other shifts; streamlining work schedules could address this. Additionally, summer months tend to reduce production by 5% due to temperature-related issues, which could be minimized by adjusting temperature control systems."

Actionable Takeaways: Practical Lessons

Over the past two years, I have worked on multiple Generative AI applications across diverse domains like procurement, finance, and HR. While AI's promise is undeniably transformative, translating that promise into real-world impact is far from straightforward. Each deployment came with its own set of challenges, opportunities, and lessons learned. In this section, I want to share my experiences and actionable insights that can help you navigate your journey with clarity and confidence.

Start Small: Building Confidence One Use Case at a Time

Organizations often aim too high, immediately attempting to apply AI to multiple complex workflows. This often leads to underwhelming results because the prompts are not tailored to specific tasks. For example, a finance team might use a generic prompt like: "*Analyse this financial report*"

Moreover, we expect AI to provide detailed insights. The result is usually too broad to be actionable.

The Solution

Start with focused, well-defined use cases and design prompts tailored to achieve clear objectives. By narrowing the scope, you can iterate quickly and refine prompts for maximum impact.

Starting with focused prompts allows teams to:

- Identify the nuances of AI responses in a controlled environment.
- Build confidence with small successes.
- Develop reusable prompts as templates for future tasks.

Encourage Experimentation: Unlock the Full Potential of Prompts

Many users treat prompts as static instructions rather than dynamic tools. For instance, in one HR project, users relied on rigid, pre-defined prompts like:
"*Write an offer letter for a new hire.*"

While functional, this approach stifled creativity and missed opportunities to customize outputs for tone, context, or audience.

The Solution

Prompt engineering thrives on experimentation. Empower teams to rephrase, restructure, and test different variations to see what works best. Please encourage them to explore advanced techniques, like chaining prompts or using multi-turn conversations to build context.

Experimentation helps teams discover how subtle changes in prompts can:

- Improve relevance and accuracy.
- Adapt outputs to different audiences.
- Inspire innovative ways to solve problems.

Document Learnings: Build a Knowledge Repository of Prompts

A lack of shared knowledge leads to inefficiencies and repeated mistakes. Different teams created similar prompts for contract reviews in one procurement project but did not share insights. This fragmented approach slowed progress and resulted in inconsistent outputs.

The Solution

Create a centralized repository to document effective prompts, learnings, and best practices.

Include details like:

- Specific use cases for each Prompt.
- Examples of what worked and what did not.
- Tips for troubleshooting ambiguous outputs.

Measure Impact: Validate the ROI of Prompt Engineering

Without measurable outcomes, it isn't easy to prove the value of prompt engineering efforts. In one finance project, leadership questioned whether fine-tuning prompts were worth the time investment, as the benefits were not immediately apparent.

The Solution

Define clear metrics to measure the impact of improved prompts. For example:

- Time saved: How much faster tasks are completed with optimized prompts.
- Accuracy: How many errors are eliminated compared to manual workflows?
- Adoption: The percentage of team members using and benefiting from the repository of prompts.

This helps to:

- Demonstrates tangible value to stakeholders.
- Builds momentum for scaling prompt engineering efforts.
- Provides data-driven insights to refine future strategies.

Every successful Generative AI deployment I have led has relied heavily on prompt engineering. Starting minor gave us the focus to create impactful solutions. Experimentation revealed untapped opportunities. Documenting learnings allowed us to scale, and measuring impact helped us prove the ROI to leadership. Prompt engineering is more than crafting instructions—it is about continuously refining and adapting to meet real-world needs. These actionable takeaways can elevate your AI efforts in procurement, finance, HR, or beyond.

Conclusion

This chapter introduced Prompt Engineering and highlighted the importance of clear and precise communication in directing Generative AI to achieve desired outcomes. It addressed fundamental concepts, including the definition of a prompt, best practices for developing effective prompts, and advanced methods such as zero-shot and chain-of-thought prompting. The chapter emphasized the value of iterative refinement and evaluation to improve prompt performance consistently. Practical examples from different domains were used to demonstrate the powerful impact of well-crafted prompts. In conclusion, the chapter portrayed prompt engineering as an essential skill for harnessing the full capabilities of AI, positioning it as a significant creative and strategic asset.

Exercise: Test Your Understanding

Answer the following questions and test your understanding of learning from

Chapter 6:

Q. 1. What is a prompt in the context of Generative AI, and why is it important?

Q. 2. What are some best practices for crafting effective prompts?

Q. 3. What is the difference between zero-shot prompting and few-shot prompting?

Q. 4. Why is iterative refinement important in prompt engineering?

Q. 5. How can advanced techniques like chain-of-thought prompt improve AI responses?

7

Frameworks to work with Azure OpenAI

Generative AI technologies, like those provided by Azure OpenAI, transform how we approach innovation. From crafting highly personalized marketing campaigns to building virtual assistants that streamline customer service, these tools unlock incredible potential. However, with this potential comes complexity.

Let us break it down:

Prompt Engineering: Every AI interaction begins with a prompt carefully crafted instruction that tells the AI model what to do. While a simple task might only need a straightforward prompt (e.g., "Summarize this paragraph"), complex applications often require layered prompts that adapt dynamically to user input or changing contexts.

For example:

- In an e-commerce chatbot, the prompt must retrieve product information, account for user preferences, and provide tailored responses.
- Managing such dynamic and context-sensitive prompts requires extensive custom coding without a proper framework.

Multi-Step Workflows: Consider an AI system designed to assist healthcare providers. A typical workflow might look like this:

- A user submits a description of symptoms.
- The system retrieves medical history from an external database.
- The AI analyzes the data and generates a response, such as potential diagnoses or next steps.
- The system sends the summary to the provider and the patient, integrating it into the clinic's existing software.
- Orchestrating such a workflow without a framework involves significant manual effort, from coordinating API calls to handling data dependencies.

Memory Management: Imagine interacting with a virtual assistant that forgets what you said moments ago. Frustrating, right? Now, picture a customer service chatbot that remembers your order history, shipping preferences, and even a previous complaint you filed.

This level of personalization is only possible with effective **memory management**—a challenging task to implement from scratch.

Seamless Integration with External Systems: AI systems rarely work in isolation. For example:
- A financial advisory chatbot should pull real-time stock market data.
- An HR assistant could require access to employee databases to answer questions about leave policies or benefits.
- Building and maintaining integrations with external APIs, databases, and third-party services can quickly become overwhelming.

The Pain Points Without a Framework

Let us visualize the effort required without a framework:

A startup wants to build an AI-powered productivity assistant using Azure OpenAI.

- **Prompt Engineering**: The developers spend weeks writing and testing prompts for different tasks, such as drafting emails, scheduling meetings, and summarizing documents.
- **Workflow Management**: To handle multi-step workflows (e.g., extracting details from an email, creating a calendar event, and sending a confirmation), they write custom logic to connect each step manually.
- **Memory Management**: They implement a system to store conversation history and recall context when needed, requiring custom database setup and optimization.
- **API Integration**: The team writes individual scripts to connect with calendar APIs, email servers, and cloud storage.

This approach delays delivery and creates brittle systems that are difficult to maintain or scale as requirements grow.

How Frameworks Solve These Problems

Open-source frameworks act like pre-built toolkits designed to handle everyday challenges so developers can focus on innovation. Here is how they help:

Efficient Workflows: Frameworks come with ready-made pipelines that allow developers to chain tasks effortlessly. For instance:

- A framework might provide an out-of-the-box workflow for a legal document analysis tool that extracts key clauses, analyzes language for compliance, and suggests edits in one seamless process.

Reusable Components: Frameworks offer libraries of reusable templates, reducing repetitive work. Imagine:

- A customer service bot framework already includes pre-built templates for prompts like "How can I help you today?" or "Please describe your issue in detail."
- Developers customize these templates to align with their business needs.

Built-In Memory Management: Instead of manually setting up a system to store and retrieve user interactions, frameworks often include memory modules. For example:

- A shopping assistant built on such a framework might automatically remember your preferences (e.g., "Always show products under $100") and reuse this information across sessions.

Seamless Integration: Frameworks simplify integration with APIs, databases, and third-party systems. For instance:

- A real estate chatbot could pull property listings from an external database and display locations using a map API—all through pre-built connectors offered by the framework.

Scalability: Frameworks are designed to handle high volumes of requests, ensuring that your AI application performs reliably even as user demand grows. A framework might provide built-in coaching, load balancing, or failover features, so developers do not need to build these systems from scratch. Open-source frameworks are not just about saving time; they fundamentally change the development experience:

- **Empower Innovation**: Developers can focus on solving real-world problems, not building infrastructure.
- **Reduce Complexity**: Common challenges like prompt engineering, workflow orchestration, and memory management are handled efficiently.
- **Ensure Quality**: Frameworks are tested by the community, ensuring robust and reliable components.
- **Encourage Collaboration**: Open-source frameworks foster collaboration, where developers can share enhancements and insights.

- With these benefits, frameworks are becoming the cornerstone of modern AI development.

Let us start by looking at some of the popular frameworks

LangChain

LangChain is a cutting-edge framework designed to simplify and optimize the development of applications powered by large language models (LLMs). It provides an ecosystem of tools, integrations, and abstractions that streamline the entire lifecycle of LLM-based applications—development, deployment, and optimization. By leveraging LangChain, developers can focus on creating innovative solutions without getting bogged down by the complexities of integrating various technologies or managing intricate workflows. LangChain is built around several foundational concepts that simplify working with LLMs and AI applications. Let us delve into the key ideas that underpin the framework:

Chat Models and Messages

- **Chat Models:** LLMs capable of processing input as sequences of messages and returning structured responses.
- **Messages:** The basic unit of communication between the user and the model, representing inputs (from users) and outputs (from the model).
- **Chat History:** A persistent conversation log that enables context-aware interactions by maintaining a sequence of alternating user inputs and model responses.

Prompt Engineering

- **Prompt Templates:** Predefined templates that standardize the static parts of prompts for reusability, versioning, and serialization.
- **Few-Shot Prompting:** A technique to improve model performance by including a few examples of tasks within the prompt.
- **Example Selectors:** Tools to dynamically select relevant examples from a dataset for effective prompting.

Memory and Multimodality

- **Memory:** Mechanisms to store and retrieve conversation history, ensuring continuity in long-running interactions.
- **Multimodality:** The ability to process diverse data types, including text, images, audio, and video, expanding the application's capabilities.

Embedding Models and Vector Stores

- **Embedding Models:** Convert data (text, images, etc.) into vector representations for efficient similarity searches.
- **Vector Stores:** Specialized databases designed for storing and retrieving these embeddings, enabling advanced retrieval-augmented generation (RAG) workflows.

Tools and Agents

- **Tools:** Functions with schemas that define their name, description, and arguments, enabling interaction with external systems.
- **Agents:** Components that use language models to decide sequences of actions (e.g., calling tools, retrieving documents) to achieve a task.

Document Handling

- **Document Loaders:** Modules to ingest external data as documents.
- **Text Splitters:** Split lengthy texts into smaller chunks for efficient indexing and retrieval.

Output Parsing and Structured Responses

- **Output Parsers:** Transform model outputs into structured formats suitable for downstream tasks.
- **Structured Output:** Techniques to make LLMs return responses in structured formats like JSON that align with predefined schemas.

Orchestration and Streaming

- **LangGraph:** A high-level orchestration tool that combines LangChain components into production-ready pipelines with persistence and streaming capabilities.
- **Streaming APIs:** Enable results to be surfaced incrementally as generated, improving interactivity and responsiveness.

Evaluation and Testing

- **Evaluation:** Assess model performance against predefined benchmarks to ensure quality and reliability.
- **Testing:** Rigorous unit and integration testing frameworks to verify the correctness of individual components and their interactions.

Semantic Kernel

Semantic Kernel is an open-source, lightweight development toolkit that empowers developers to incorporate advanced AI models into their applications seamlessly. Designed for C#, Python, and Java, it acts as middleware that accelerates the delivery of enterprise-grade solutions by bridging the gap between AI capabilities and existing codebases.

At its core, Semantic Kernel enables AI agents to interact with your application's functionalities by combining natural language prompts with your existing APIs. By describing your code to AI models, the framework can interpret requests, invoke the appropriate functions, and return the results, creating a seamless flow between AI and application logic.

Key Features and Components of Semantic Kernel

In this section, we will discuss the Key features and components of Semantic Kernel in details:

The Kernel: The Central Component

The Kernel is the backbone of the Semantic Kernel, acting as a Dependency Injection (DI) container that manages services and plugins essential for running AI-driven applications. Developers can register all required services and plugins with the Kernel, enabling the AI to utilize them as needed without manual intervention.

AI Service Connectors

Semantic Kernel provides a unified abstraction layer to interact with various AI services from multiple providers. These services include:

- **Chat Completion:** Enabling conversational AI interactions.
- **Text Generation:** Crafting creative or informative text.
- **Embedding Generation:** Creating vector representations of data.
- **Multimodal AI Services:** These include Text-to-Image, Image-to-Text, Text-to-Audio, and Audio-to-Text.

This standard interface simplifies switching between AI providers and ensures flexibility in development.

Vector Store Connectors

The framework supports connectors for vector stores and specialized databases for storing and searching vector embeddings. While Semantic Kernel does not automatically use a vector store, developers can expose vector search capabilities as plugins, making them available to AI models for retrieval-augmented generation (RAG) tasks.

Functions and Plugins

Plugins in Semantic Kernel serve as named containers for functions. These functions can:

- **Be exposed to the AI:** Allowing the model to invoke them dynamically.
- **Be called within templates:** Providing predefined actions during template execution.

This modular design enhances reusability and promotes a clean separation of concerns.

Prompt Templates

Prompt templates combine instructions, user input, and function outputs into a cohesive structure. For example, a template might:

- Include detailed instructions for an AI model.
- Incorporate placeholders for user input.
- Hardcode calls to specific plugins that need execution before engaging the AI model.

This capability empowers developers and prompts engineers to create highly customizable interactions.

Filters

Filters enable developers to define custom actions that execute at specific stages of the chat completion workflow, including:

- Before or after function invocation.

- Before or after prompt rendering.

By registering filters with the Kernel, developers gain fine-grained control over AI behavior and integration workflows.

Agent Framework

Semantic Kernel's Agent Framework facilitates the creation of AI agents and the integration of agentic patterns into applications. These agents leverage the Kernel's core features—like plugins and prompt templates—to make autonomous decisions, execute actions, and enhance business processes.

Semantic Kernel simplifies the integration of cutting-edge AI technologies into diverse applications. Here is why it stands out:

- **Ease of Use:** The middleware architecture minimizes the complexity of calling AI models and integrating them with existing APIs.
- **Flexibility:** Its modular design allows developers to use components independently or in combination, tailoring the framework to specific needs.
- **Scalability:** Semantic Kernel's abstraction layers make it easy to switch between AI providers, integrate vector stores, and adapt to changing business requirements.
- **Enterprise-Ready:** Designed for scalability and reliability, it is an ideal solution for building AI-powered enterprise applications.

Criteria for Selecting an AI Framework: Tailoring Choices to Your Needs

Choosing the proper framework is a critical step in developing AI-powered applications. With numerous options available, evaluating frameworks based on how well they align with your specific project requirements and goals is essential.

Here are four key criteria to guide your decision:

Project Goals and Scope

Your chosen framework should directly support your project's objectives and scale to meet its demands. Consider the following:

- **Define Core Objectives:** Are you building a chatbot, automating workflows, or integrating AI with existing systems? Identify frameworks specialized for your use case.
- **Scalability:** Opt for frameworks that efficiently handle increased complexity and user load for large-scale projects or those expected to grow.
- **Functionality Needs:** Determine whether the framework supports advanced features like conversation memory, multimodal inputs, or integration with external APIs and databases.

Compatibility with Existing Systems

Integration with your current tech stack is crucial for a seamless development experience and to maximize ROI on your existing infrastructure. Evaluate frameworks for:

- **Language Support:** Ensure the framework is compatible with your primary programming language (e.g., Python, C#, Java).
- **API and Database Integration:** Look for built-in connectors or support for integrating with your APIs, databases, and third-party tools.
- **Cloud vs. On-Premises:** Decide if you require cloud-native solutions or frameworks that can run on-premise for tighter control over data and infrastructure.
- **Ease of Migration:** If migrating from an existing AI solution, prioritize frameworks that simplify the transition.

Ease of Use and Learning Curve

A framework should be developer-friendly to minimize the time spent learning and implementing it. Factors to consider include:

- **User-Friendly APIs:** Frameworks with intuitive APIs and apparent abstractions can reduce development effort.
- **Pre-Built Components:** Look for pre-built workflows, templates, and tools to accelerate development.
- **Documentation and Tutorials:** Comprehensive, well-organized documentation and beginner-friendly tutorials can significantly reduce the learning curve.
- **Setup and Maintenance:** Consider frameworks that are easy to set up, configure, and maintain, especially for smaller teams.

Community Support and Documentation

The strength of a framework's community and the quality of its support resources can significantly impact your development experience. Look for:

- **Active Community:** An active user base ensures timely answers to queries and access to shared knowledge.
- **Frequent Updates:** A well-maintained framework with regular updates reflects the commitment of its developers.
- **Third-Party Integrations:** Strong ecosystems often support many integrations and extensions.
- **Support Channels:** Availability of forums, GitHub issues, Slack groups, or other direct support options.
- **Case Studies and Success Stories:** These can provide insight into how the framework performs in real-world scenarios.

Conclusion

Selecting the proper AI framework involves balancing your project's goals with practical considerations like system compatibility, ease of use, and available support. By evaluating frameworks based on these criteria, you can make an informed choice that aligns with your development needs and ensures the success of your AI application.

Exercise: Test Your Understanding

Answer the following questions and test your understanding of learning from

`Chapter 7`:

`Q. 1.` What are the primary considerations when choosing between LangChain and Semantic Kernel for an AI project?

`Q. 2.` How does LangChain simplify the development of applications powered by large language models (LLMs)?

`Q. 3.` Describe the role of the Kernel in the Semantic Kernel framework?

`Q. 4.` What are the key benefits of using frameworks like LangChain and Semantic Kernel for building AI solutions?

`Q. 5.` Explain the importance of prompt engineering in modern AI solutions and how it is managed within LangChain?

8

Multi-Agent Framework and Design Principles

At the crossroads of artificial intelligence and creativity, a transformative concept is emerging—one that is revolutionizing industries and unlocking new dimensions of problem-solving and innovation. This concept, Generative AI agents, represents a paradigm shift in which intelligence is no longer confined to analyzing and processing data. Instead, it extends to creating and generating new solutions, ideas, and products.

A Generative AI agent is an autonomous entity powered by artificial intelligence that does not just provide information—it actively performs actions. These agents go beyond performing predefined tasks based on fixed instructions. Instead, they generate novel outputs or solutions in text, images, code, music, designs, or complex strategies. Their defining characteristic is their ability to produce something new, often guided by patterns, rules, or learned experiences from vast amounts of data.

Think of them as digital creators: Generative AI agents can draw inspiration from existing information, but they can combine, evolve, and invent new outcomes that are not merely derivative of the data they were trained on.

Now that we understand Generative AI agents and their ability to create, innovate, and solve complex problems, we must explore how these agents can evolve from solitary creators to a collaborative ecosystem. This shift from a single agent to a multi-agent approach opens the door to unprecedented possibilities. It is not just about one Agent performing a task; it is about multiple agents working together, exchanging information, negotiating, and collectively reaching goals that no single agent could achieve alone.

The Emergence of Multi-Agent Systems (MAS)

Single-agent systems are highly effective within well-defined, predictable tasks. However, the single Agent faces inherent challenges when the problem space grows more complex, dynamic, and interconnected.

This is where multi-agent systems (MAS) come into play. Rather than relying on a single agent to solve all the problems, a multi-agent system is designed to use multiple autonomous agents that work together to achieve shared objectives. In a MAS, each Agent brings expertise, learns from its environment, and collaborates or competes with other agents to solve complex, multi-faceted challenges.

In the context of Generative AI-based agents, multi-agent systems extend the concept of individual agents into a dynamic, collaborative ecosystem. Each Agent in the system performs specialized tasks, learns from interactions, and communicates with others to solve more significant, complex problems.

Why Multi-Agent Systems are the Future of Generative AI

The key advantage of **multi-agent systems** is that they enable **scalability, resilience, and adaptability** in ways that single-agent systems cannot. As the world becomes more interconnected and dynamic, problems become more complex. Single-agent systems struggle when the environment is uncertain, requires multi-faceted expertise, or change rapidly.

A **multi-agent system** provides a framework where agents can:

- **Collaborate** to solve complex problems by pooling their expertise and capabilities.
- **Adapt** to changing circumstances through negotiation, learning, and real-time communication.
- **Scale** quickly by adding more agents to handle new tasks, domains, or areas of expertise without disrupting the entire system.

Key Characteristics of Multi-Agent Systems (MAS)

Multi-agent systems (MAS) are designed to solve complex, dynamic problems by leveraging the capabilities of multiple autonomous agents that work together to achieve common or competing goals. Each Agent in a MAS is independent but interacts with others to contribute to the system's overall objectives. Below are the core characteristics that define **Multi-Agent Systems**:

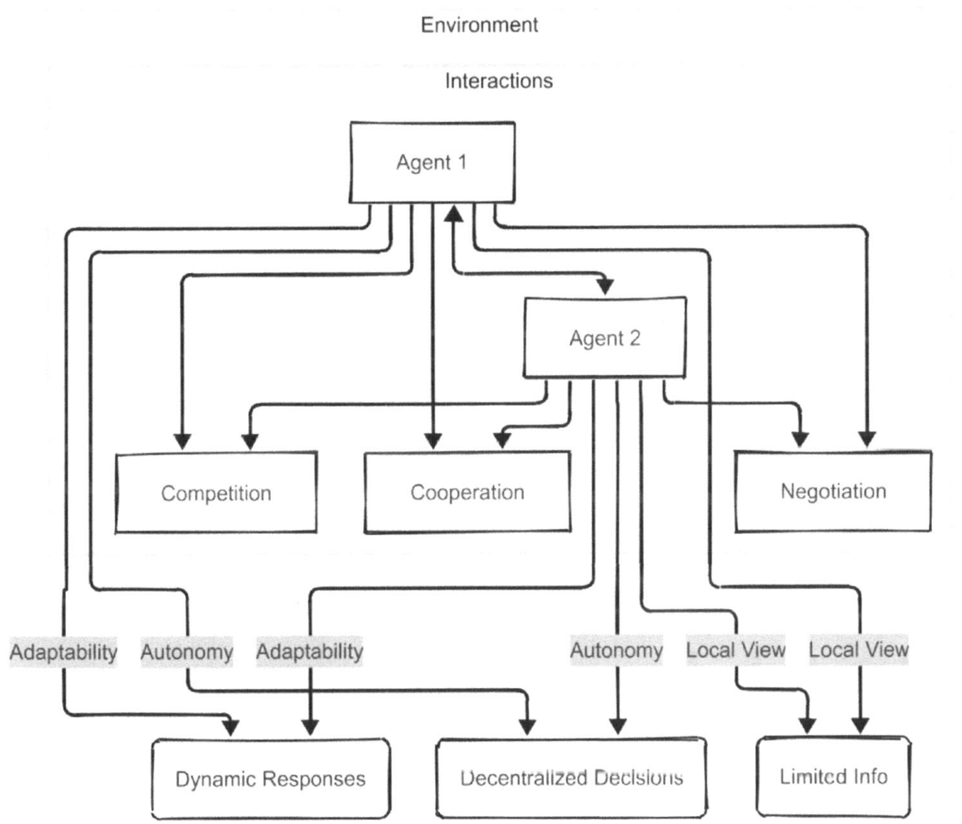

Fig 8.1: MAS accessibility with Agent and environment

The above image illustrates the key characteristics and interactions of Multi-Agent Systems (MAS), focusing on Agent 1 and Agent 2. It showcases the agents' autonomy, local view, adaptability, and interactions: cooperation, competition, and negotiation. Each characteristic is connected to its corresponding description.

Autonomy

Agents in a MAS are **autonomous**, meaning they can make decisions and take actions independently based on their internal processes without direct control from an external source.

This autonomy allows agents to operate effectively in decentralized environments, making them ideal for scenarios where a central controller would be inefficient or impractical. For instance, in a **smart city**, autonomous agents might manage traffic, public transportation, and utilities, each making decisions based on real-time data, all without a central command.

Local Views

Each Agent has a **local view** of the environment, meaning it has limited information about the overall system or the state of other agents.

This characteristic promotes scalability, as agents do not need a global perspective. Instead, they focus on their knowledge and tasks, sharing information when necessary. For example, in **supply chain management**, a procurement agent might only know about a specific set of suppliers but communicate with other agents for inventory, shipping, and demand forecasts.

Decentralized Control

A MAS has no central controller; control is distributed across the agents. Each Agent makes decisions based on its information and interactions with other agents.

Decentralized control increases the system's scalability and robustness. If one Agent fails, others can adjust and continue functioning, ensuring the system remains resilient. For instance, in **robotic swarms**, where robots autonomously complete tasks like exploration or surveillance, others compensate without disrupting the system's performance if one robot malfunctions.

Adaptability

Agents in MAS can adapt their behavior in response to changes in their environment, goals, or the actions of other agents. This adaptability allows MAS to operate in dynamic, unpredictable environments where conditions change rapidly, such as **disaster response** or **real-time resource allocation**. For example, an agent managing emergency responses might change its strategy based on weather conditions or new information about the disaster.

Interaction

Agents interact through various forms of communication—whether directly or indirectly.

These interactions can include cooperation, competition, and negotiation.

- **Cooperation**: Agents collaborate to achieve common goals, sharing resources or strategies.
- **Competition**: Agents with conflicting goals may act strategically to optimize their outcomes, potentially competing for resources.
- **Negotiation**: Agents may negotiate to resolve conflicts, allocate resources, or make joint decisions.

These interactions are crucial for achieving global system objectives and resolving conflicts. For example, energy distribution agents may cooperate to balance the power supply in an intelligent grid system. However, some agents may negotiate during peak demand to prioritize specific consumers or sectors.

Multi-Agent Conversation Patterns

As multi-agent systems evolve, their ability to interact effectively through structured conversation patterns becomes critical. Conversations in multi-agent systems are not merely information exchanges but coordination, negotiation, collaboration, and decision-making mechanisms. Depending on the system's requirements, these conversation patterns range from simple two-agent exchanges to more complex hierarchical, dynamic, or nested interactions.

Below is an exploration of various multi-agent conversation patterns:

Direct Two-Agent Conversations

The simplest form of multi-agent interaction is a two-agent conversation, where two autonomous agents communicate directly to achieve a specific goal or exchange information.

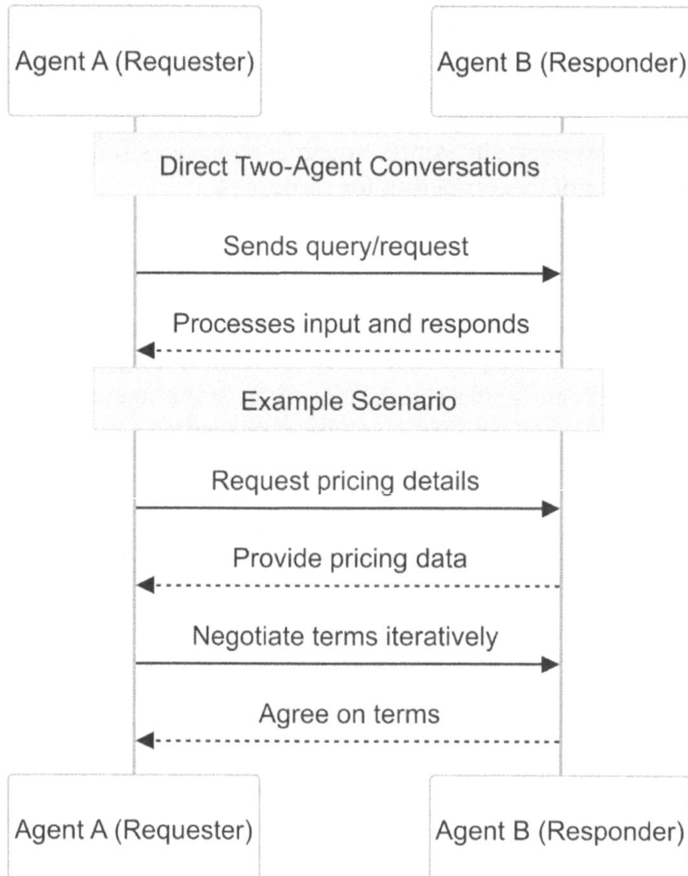

Fig 8.2 Direct Two-Agent Conversations

This image illustrates a direct two-agent interaction in which Agent A (Requester) communicates with Agent B (Responder) to achieve a goal. It depicts a procurement scenario in which Agent A requests pricing details, Agent B provides the data, and they negotiate terms iteratively.

Structure

- Agent A sends a query or a request.
- Agent B processes the input and responds.

Example: in a procurement scenario, a **price negotiation agent** (Agent A) may request pricing details from a **supplier agent** (Agent B). The supplier agent provides the requested data, and they negotiate terms iteratively.

This pattern is efficient for straightforward interactions requiring minimal complexity but can struggle in dynamic or multi-faceted tasks requiring broader coordination.

Coordinated Multi-Agent Conversations

In scenarios where multiple agents must collaborate, diverse communication patterns emerge based on task complexity, hierarchy, and decision-making requirements.

Hierarchical Conversations

In hierarchical conversations, agents interact within a predefined structure where a **lead agent** manages and consolidates input from subordinate agents.

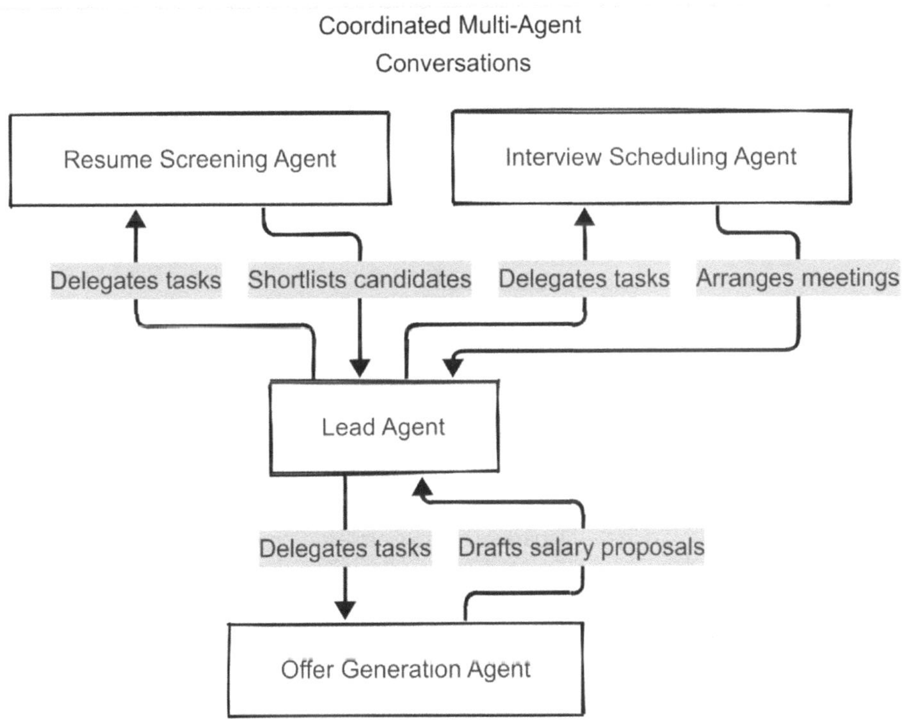

Fig 8.3 Hierarchical Conversations in Coordinated Multi-Agent Systems

This image visually represents the hierarchical conversation structure in coordinated multi-agent systems, clearly understanding how tasks are delegated and synthesized in a collaborative environment.

Structure:

- A lead agent oversees the conversation, delegating specific tasks to supporting agents and synthesizing their outputs.

Example: in **HR recruitment**, a **central recruiter agent** could coordinate with:

- A **resume screening agent** to shortlist candidates.
- An **interview scheduling agent** will arrange meetings with managers.
- An **offer generation agent** to draft salary proposals.

By centralizing control, this pattern simplifies the user's interaction and ensures seamless task execution across multiple specialized agents.

Dynamic Group Conversations

Dynamic group conversations offer flexibility by allowing multiple agents to interact fluidly without a strict hierarchy.

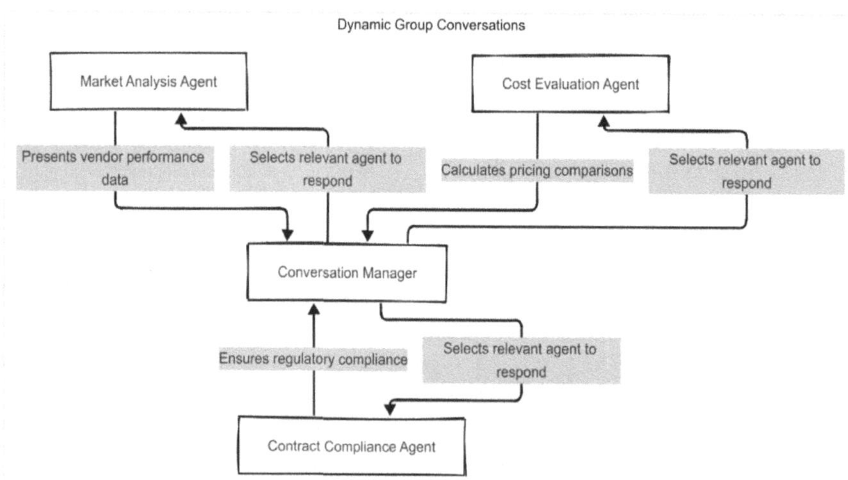

Fig 8.4 Dynamic Group Conversations

This image visually represents the dynamic group conversation structure in multi-agent systems, illustrating how the conversation manager facilitates fluid and context-based interactions among multiple agents.

Structure

- A **conversation manager** oversees the group, broadcasting messages and selecting the most relevant Agent to respond based on context or expertise.

Example: in **procurement**, a **supplier selection conversation** might involve:

- A **market analysis agent** presenting vendor performance data.
- A **cost evaluation agent** calculating pricing comparisons.
- A **contract compliance agent** ensuring regulatory requirements are met.

The conversation manager ensures that the right Agent speaks at the right time, enabling efficient and dynamic decision-making.

Nested Conversations

Nested conversations involve breaking down complex tasks into **sub-conversations,** with agents diving into specific areas of expertise before returning to the main discussion.

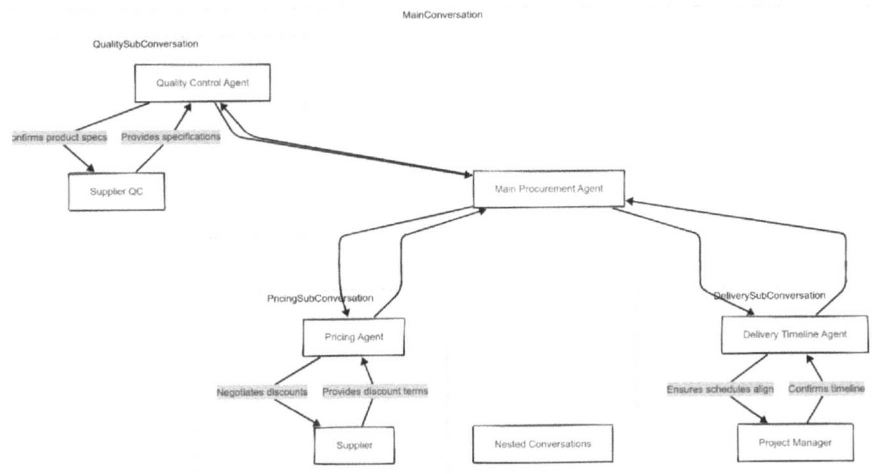

Fig 8.5 Nested Conversations

This image visually represents the nested conversation structure in multi-agent systems, illustrating how complex tasks are broken down into sub-conversations for thorough and multi-faceted problem-solving.

Structure

- Agents engage in sub-discussions to resolve granular issues and contribute to the conversation.

Example: in **procurement**, a negotiation process might involve:

- A **pricing agent** negotiating discounts with suppliers.
- A **delivery timeline agent** ensures schedules align with project deadlines.
- A **quality control agent** confirming product specifications.

These sub-conversations are nested within the broader procurement strategy discussion, enabling thorough and multi-faceted problem-solving.

Conversations with Varying Levels

of Autonomy

Multi-agent systems must also balance **autonomy** and **human involvement** to suit the complexity and criticality of the task.

- **Entirely Autonomous Conversations**: Agents communicate and make decisions independently.
  Example: In **finance**, autonomous trading agents can interact and execute trades based on market conditions without human intervention.
- **Human-in-the-Loop Conversations**: Agents collaborate with humans at decision points, seeking input or approval.
  Example: In **HR**, agents might shortlist candidates autonomously but require human confirmation before extending interview invitations.
- **Human-Guided Conversations**: Humans lead the conversation, and agents assist by providing insights or automating subtasks.
  Example: In **procurement**, a human manager might guide the negotiation while agents fetch data on pricing trends or legal requirements.

Challenges in Multi-Agent Conversations

- **Coordination Complexity**: Managing transitions and ensuring coherence in multi-agent interactions.
- **Conflict Resolution**: Designing mechanisms to address competing goals among agents.
- **Scalability**: Maintaining system performance as the number of agents and interactions grows.

Opportunities in Multi-Agent Conversations

- **Efficiency**: Structured conversation patterns reduce time and effort for complex tasks.
- **Flexibility**: Dynamic and nested patterns allow agents to adapt to changing conditions.
- **Enhanced Collaboration**: By enabling multi-agent interactions, systems can tackle problems that require diverse expertise

Coordination and Collaboration in Multi-Agent Systems

Coordination and collaboration are fundamental to multi-agent systems (MAS) success. These systems consist of autonomous agents working together to achieve shared objectives, resolve conflicts, and adapt to dynamic environments. In the context of **Generative AI-enhanced Multi-Agent Systems**, these capabilities are taken to a new level, enabling more sophisticated interactions, creative problem-solving, and seamless integration into real-world applications.

Techniques for Coordination in Multi-Agent Systems

In this section, we will discuss various techniques of Multi-Agent Systems.

Task Allocation

Task allocation involves distributing tasks among agents to optimize system performance. This can be achieved using various methods:

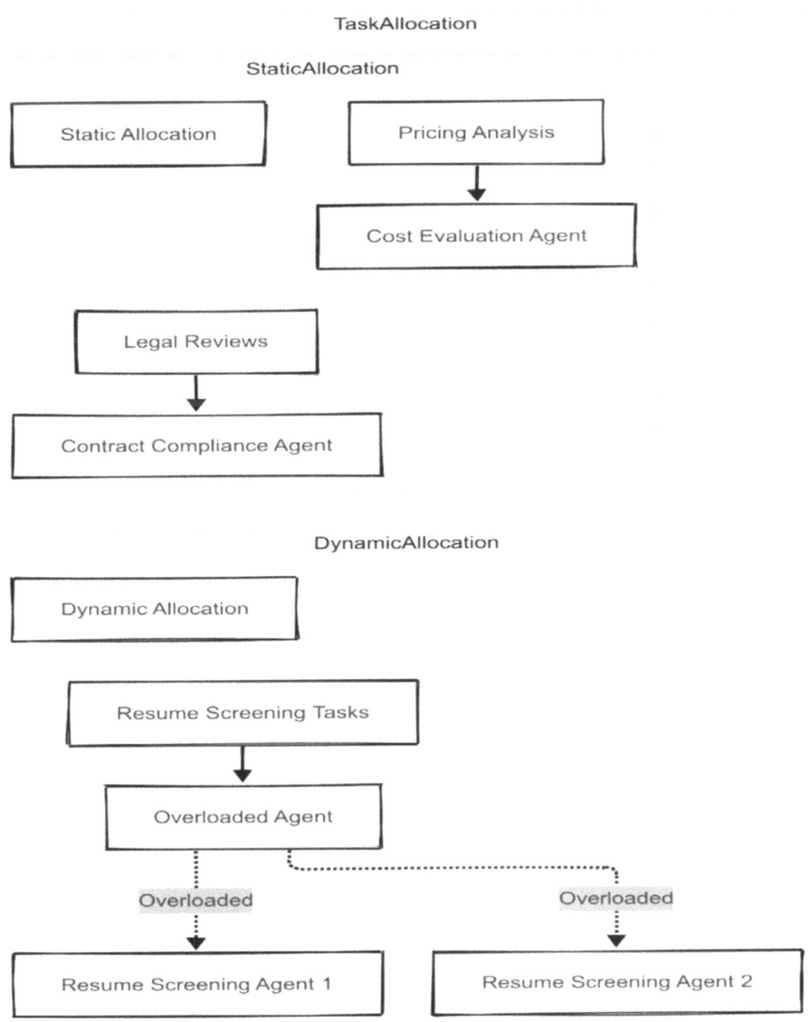

Fig 8.6: MAS agent support to resolve complicated task assignments

This image illustrates two task allocation methods in multi-agent systems: static and dynamic. In static allocation, tasks are assigned to agents based on predefined roles or expertise, such as a contract compliance agent handling legal reviews and a cost evaluation agent focusing on pricing analysis. In dynamic allocation, tasks are assigned based on real-time conditions and agent availability; for instance, if a resume-screening agent becomes overloaded, tasks can dynamically shift to another available agent to optimize performance.

- **Static Allocation**: Tasks are assigned to agents based on predefined roles or expertise.
  Example: A contract compliance agent handles legal reviews in procurement, while a cost evaluation agent focuses on pricing analysis.
- **Dynamic Allocation**: Tasks are assigned based on real-time conditions, agent availability, or performance metrics.
  Example: In **HR recruitment**, if one resume-screening Agent becomes overloaded, tasks can dynamically shift to another agent

Goal Alignment

Goal alignment ensures that all agents in the system work towards a common objective, even when their individual goals may differ.

Methods

- **Global Objectives**: Defining overarching goals that guide agent behavior.
- **Incentive Mechanisms**: Reward structures that encourage agents to prioritize shared goals.
- **Consensus Algorithms**: Protocols like leader election or voting to align agents on critical decisions.

Example: In **finance**, agents involved in portfolio management (e.g., risk evaluation, asset allocation, and performance tracking agents) align their outputs to maximize the portfolio's overall return while minimizing risk.

Conflict Resolution

Conflict resolution is critical when agents have competing priorities, limited resources, or overlapping tasks.

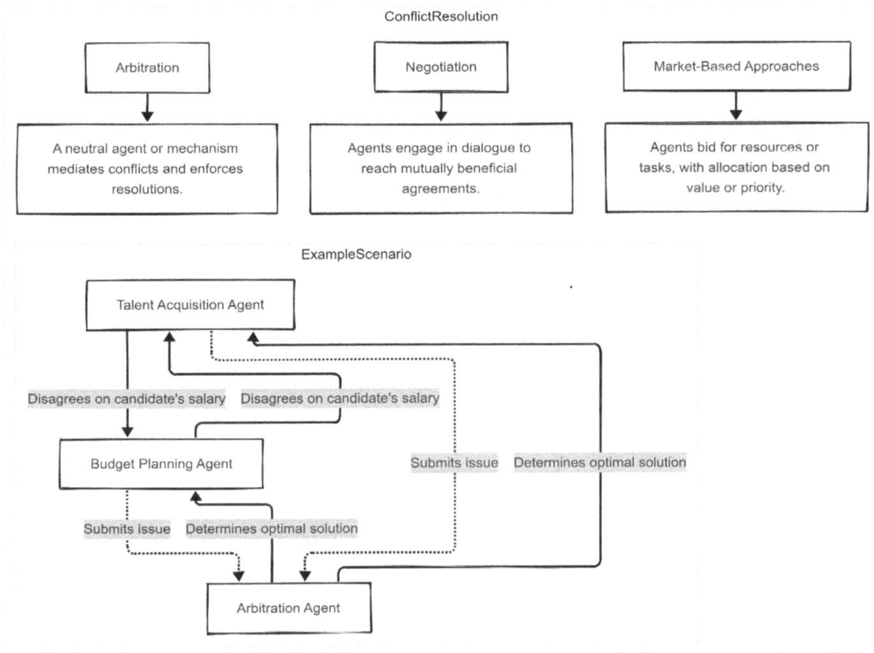

Fig 8.7: Conflict resolution through agents

This image illustrates conflict resolution techniques among agents, including negotiation, arbitration, and market-based approaches. In an example HR scenario, if a talent acquisition agent and a budget planning agent disagree on a candidate's salary package, a neutral arbitration agent mediates the conflict to determine an optimal solution based on organizational priorities.

Techniques

- **Negotiation**: Agents engage in dialogue to reach mutually beneficial agreements.
- **Arbitration**: A neutral agent or mechanism mediates conflicts and enforces resolutions.
- **Market-Based Approaches**: Agents "bid" for resources or tasks, with allocation based on value or priority.

Example: In **HR**, if two agents (e.g., a talent acquisition agent and a budget planning agent) disagree on a candidate's salary package, a third agent or arbitration process can determine the optimal solution based on organizational priorities.

Multi-Agent System Architectures Considerations

Multi-agent systems (MAS) thrive on their architecture—the structural blueprint determining how agents interact, communicate, and collaborate to achieve collective goals. When infused with **Generative AI**, these architectures gain enhanced adaptability, creativity, and decision-making capabilities. Let us explore the major types of architectures—centralized, decentralized, and hybrid—and how Generative AI influences them, focusing on scalability and fault tolerance.

Centralized Architecture

In centralized architecture, a single **central agent or hub** oversees the operations and communication of all other agents in the system.

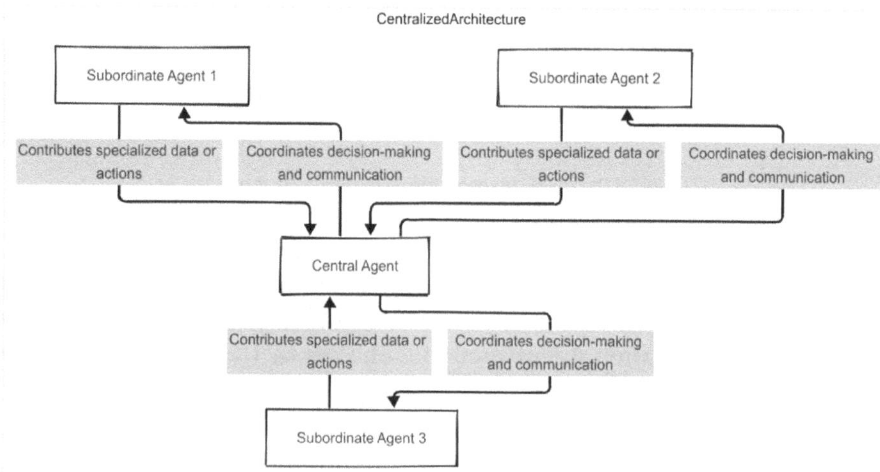

Fig 8.8: Centralized agent architecture

This image illustrates centralized architecture in a multi-agent system. A central agent oversees all operations and communication. Subordinate agents contribute specialized data or actions to the central Agent, coordinating decision-making. While this structure offers simplified management and easy implementation, it faces challenges such as a single point of failure and limited scalability.

Structure

- The central Agent coordinates decision-making and communication.
- Other agents act as subordinates, contributing specialized data or actions to the central Agent.

Advantages
- Simplified management and oversight.
- Easy to implement and monitor.

Challenges
- Single point of failure: The system collapses if the central Agent fails.
- Limited scalability: Adding more agents can overwhelm the central Agent.

Decentralized Architecture

In decentralized architectures, agents operate autonomously, with no central entity controlling their interactions. Decisions emerge from distributed communication and collaboration among agents.

Structure
- Each Agent has equal status and makes decisions based on local information and interactions with other agents.
- Communication and decision-making are distributed.

Advantages
- High fault tolerance: Failure of one Agent does not disrupt the system.
- Excellent scalability: Adding more agents does not bottleneck the system.

Challenges
- Coordination complexity: Ensuring coherence across agents is challenging without a central agent.
- More significant resource usage: Requires robust communication protocols to maintain efficiency.

Hybrid Architecture

Hybrid architecture combines features of centralized and decentralized models, providing flexibility in task allocation and decision-making.

Structure
- A central entity exists but only coordinates specific high-level tasks or strategic decisions.
- Autonomous agents handle localized tasks and collaborate independently.

Advantages
- Balances the strengths of centralized and decentralized models.
- Enhanced fault tolerance and scalability compared to purely centralized systems.

Challenges
- Balancing autonomy and central control can introduce design complexity.
- Requires sophisticated communication protocols to integrate centralized and decentralized components.

Key Design Principles for Multi-Agent AI Solutions

Designing multi-agent AI systems is both an art and a science. It requires a deep understanding of how intelligent agents can work harmoniously and efficiently while addressing real-world challenges such as scalability, communication, adaptability, and security. Throughout my experience working with AI-driven automation, I have seen firsthand how overlooking these principles can lead to inefficiencies, system failures, and even ethical dilemmas. Below, I summarize the key design principles that are the foundation for building robust, scalable, and intelligent multi-agent AI solutions.

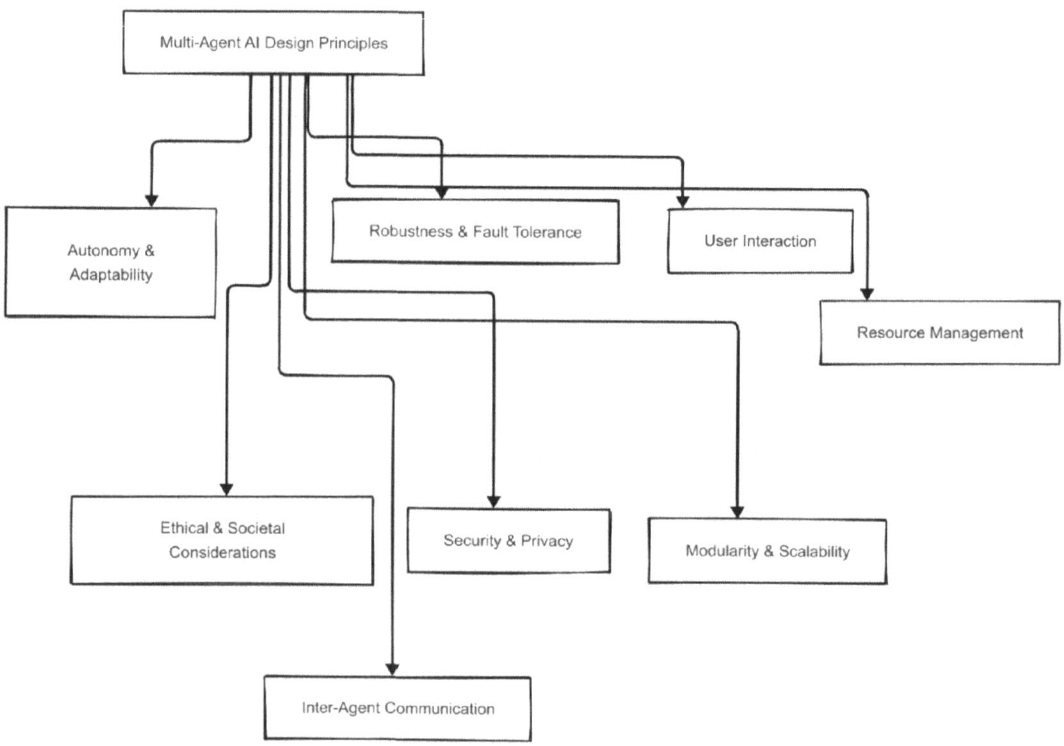

Fig 8.9 Key Design Principles for Multi-Agent AI Systems

This image illustrates the eight fundamental design principles for developing robust, scalable, intelligent multi-agent AI systems. Each principle—modularity and scalability, Communication, Autonomy, Robustness, Resource Management, Security, User Interaction, and Ethics—is crucial in ensuring efficiency, adaptability, and responsible AI deployment.

Modularity and Scalability: Building for Growth

One of the biggest mistakes I have seen in AI system design is the temptation to build monolithic architectures where every Agent is deeply intertwined with others. This not only creates a maintenance nightmare but also hinders scalability. Instead, a modular approach allows each Agent to function as an independent yet cooperative unit.

- **Modularity:** Think of each Agent as a LEGO brick—designed to fit seamlessly with others but also replaceable and adaptable to new structures. A modular system enables developers to update, test, or remove specific agents without affecting the entire ecosystem.
- **Scalability:** Multi-agent systems must be designed to scale efficiently. In my early projects, we underestimated the impact of agent population growth, which led to bottlenecks and degraded performance. Using distributed architectures, parallel processing, and cloud-native solutions ensures that the system can dynamically handle an increasing number of agents.

Inter-Agent Communication: Enabling Seamless Coordination

Effective communication is the glue that holds everything together in a multi-agent system. Without it, agents operate in silos, leading to inefficiencies and missed opportunities.

- **Communication Protocols:** Establishing standardized protocols ensures that agents can communicate reliably, regardless of their function or origin. Whether it is JSON-based APIs, MQTT for IoT agents, or natural language protocols for AI chatbots, ensuring compatibility is crucial.
- **Coordination Mechanisms:** In my experience, systems that lack structured coordination mechanisms end up in chaos—agents working against each other or overloading shared resources. Implementing negotiation strategies, blackboard architectures, or consensus algorithms (such as the Paxos or Raft protocols) helps synchronize actions among agents efficiently.

Autonomy and Adaptability: Intelligence Beyond Predefined Rules

A powerful multi-agent AI system does not require constant human intervention. Instead, agents should be capable of making decisions independently while adapting to their environment.

- **Autonomy:** Agents should be designed to make localized decisions based on available data, objectives, and constraints. Over-reliance on centralized control can create bottlenecks and failure points.
- **Adaptability:** The best AI systems evolve. In one of my projects, we initially hardcoded decision rules for our agents, but we quickly realized that static rules could not handle real-world complexity. By integrating reinforcement learning and self-learning mechanisms, we allowed agents to adjust their behavior based on experience and feedback.

Robustness and Fault Tolerance: Designing for the Unexpected

No system is immune to failures. Whether it is a network outage, hardware failure, or unexpected agent behavior, a multi-agent AI system must be designed to handle disruptions gracefully.

- **Robustness:** The system should be resilient to individual agent failures. For instance, if one chatbot in a customer service ecosystem goes down, others should seamlessly take over.
- **Fault Tolerance:** Redundancy and failover mechanisms are key. Techniques such as distributed control, agent replication, and checkpoint-based recovery help prevent single points of failure.

Resource Management: Maximizing Efficiency in a Shared Environment

In multi-agent systems, resources such as computing power, memory, and bandwidth must be managed efficiently to prevent contention and ensure smooth operation.

- **Efficient Resource Allocation:** Optimization algorithms, such as game-theoretic approaches and market-based allocation, help balance resource usage.

- **Conflict Resolution:** Arbitration techniques (such as priority scheduling or bidding systems) can resolve conflicts fairly when multiple agents compete for the same resource.

Security and Privacy: Safeguarding the System

As AI systems become more interconnected, security and privacy concerns grow exponentially. A breach in one Agent can compromise the entire system.

- **Security:** Encryption, authentication, and anomaly detection mechanisms should be baked into the system design from the outset.
- **Privacy:** Protecting sensitive data is critical, especially in healthcare and finance applications. Privacy-preserving AI techniques, such as differential privacy and federated learning, can help mitigate risks.

User Interaction and Interface: Bridging AI and Human Users

Even the most advanced multi-agent system is useless if users cannot interact with it effectively.

- **User-Friendly Interfaces:** Dashboards, visualization tools, and interactive controls help users monitor and guide agent behavior.
- **Feedback Mechanisms:** Continuous learning from user feedback ensures the system evolves according to user needs.

Ethical and Societal Considerations: Designing for Greater Good

Multi-agent AI systems do not operate in a vacuum—they impact real people, industries, and societies. Ethical considerations must be at the forefront of design.

- **Ethical Behavior:** AI agents should have ethical constraints to prevent harmful actions, bias, or manipulation.
- **Social Impact:** Before deploying multi-agent AI at scale, assessing risks and ensuring that it benefits society is critical.

Developing a multi-agent AI system is like orchestrating a symphony—each Agent plays its part, but the true magic happens when everything works together seamlessly. By focusing on modularity, scalability, communication, adaptability, robustness, resource efficiency, security, user experience, and ethics, developers can create AI ecosystems that are not only technically sound but also impactful and responsible. By integrating these principles, we are moving closer to building AI solutions that are not only smart but also resilient, ethical, and future proof.

Applications of Multi-Agent Generative AI

The versatility and power of **Multi-Agent Generative AI** have led to its adoption across various industries, enhancing capabilities from real-time decision-making to complex problem-solving. These systems transform key finance, healthcare, procurement, HR, and transportation processes by enabling agents to work autonomously, interact intelligently, and generate creative solutions. Below is an in-depth look at how Multi-Agent Generative AI revolutionizes these fields.

Healthcare: Coordinating Patient Care

Multi-agent systems help healthcare providers deliver personalized patient care by autonomously coordinating tasks across multiple healthcare professionals and systems.

How it works: Multiple agents represent healthcare entities—doctors, nurses, administrative staff, and external specialists. They communicate and collaborate to ensure that patients receive timely and effective care. Generative AI can help the system optimize workflows, generate care plans, and recommend interventions based on real-time data.

Example: A system of agents can autonomously schedule patient appointments, prioritize cases based on urgency, and generate follow-up treatment suggestions. If a patient's condition worsens, an AI agent might initiate emergency alerts and coordinate actions across care teams.

Benefit: It ensures timely, coordinated care, enhances workflow efficiency, reduces human error, and improves patient outcomes.

Procurement: Collaborative Supplier Selection

How it works: Multiple agents work together to simulate different **supplier scenarios**. Each Agent focuses on different factors (e.g., cost, lead time, quality) and communicates with others to determine the most optimal supplier for the buyer. Agents generate different procurement plans and negotiate terms autonomously.

Example: One Agent may generate a list of potential suppliers based on cost and quality, another focuses on delivery timelines, and a third evaluates long-term relationships or reputations. The agents then collaborate by combining these factors into a final selection strategy that optimizes the buyer's objectives.

Benefit: A more thorough, data-driven, and dynamic supplier selection process, where agents share insights and strategies to ensure the best choice.

Human Resources (HR): Collaborative Employee Engagement

How it works: In a **multi-agent HR system**, agents simulate various aspects of employee engagement, including job satisfaction, career development, and benefits optimization. These agents work together to generate personalized engagement strategies that adapt to individual needs and evolving company goals.

Example: One Agent may simulate feedback from employee satisfaction surveys, while another generates targeted career development programs based on employee performance data. A third agent tracks work-life balance trends and recommends strategies for improvement.

Benefit: A more personalized and adaptive approach to employee engagement, helping HR teams retain talent and improve job satisfaction by continuously optimizing their strategies

Conclusion

This chapter delves into the transformative concept of multi-agent systems (MAS) and the foundational design principles underpinning these sophisticated AI frameworks. The exploration began with an introduction to the burgeoning field of Generative AI agents, which are not merely passive data processors but active creators capable of generating novel solutions across various domains. This innovation marks a paradigm shift, leading us to consider the next evolution—multi-agent systems where these generative agents collaborate, communicate, and coalesce to tackle more complex, dynamic problems than ever before.

The future of multi-agent generative AI is promising, with potential advancements poised to revolutionize various sectors further. As these systems evolve, they will become even more integral to solving complex, dynamic problems that require diverse expertise and real-time adaptability. By leveraging the power of collaborative, autonomous agents, we can unlock new dimensions of innovation and efficiency, paving the way for more intelligent, resilient, and adaptive AI systems. The applications of MAS have been identified as highly prominent not only in academics/research but also in industry. The use cases and their applicability are increasing. The MAS systems are needed for the future, and the more they are used, the more benefits they will have.

Exercise: Test Your Understanding

Answer the following questions and test your understanding of learning from

Chapter 8:

Q. 1. What are multi-agent conversations' main challenges and opportunities within multi-agent systems?

Q. 2. What are the primary benefits of using Multi-Agent Systems (MAS) over single-agent systems?

Q. 3. Describe the core characteristics of Multi-Agent Systems (MAS)?

Q. 4. What are the three main types of conversation patterns in Multi-Agent Systems, and how do they function?

Q. 5. Explain the significance of modularity and scalability in designing Multi-Agent AI systems?

9

Applying Generative AI Solutions for Horizontal Functions

Over the years, working on digital transformation projects across industries, I have had the privilege of sitting at the table with leaders from Procurement, HR, Legal, and Finance. These experiences have brought me face-to-face with the people behind the processes—Procurement leaders battling tight deadlines, HR professionals striving to foster an inclusive culture, Legal teams navigating a sea of contracts, and Finance departments working tirelessly to keep the numbers aligned. Each conversation carried a common thread: These leaders sought tools and solutions to simplify their lives and empower their teams to focus on what truly matters. These are the functions that keep an organization running like a well-oiled machine. However, I have witnessed the challenges these teams face repeatedly, the manual, repetitive processes, the hours spent searching for insights buried in a mountain of data, and the constant struggle to do more with less. I vividly recall a meeting with a Procurement director at a global retail company. She spoke with exhaustion, describing how her team spent weeks manually reviewing contracts to identify risks and ensure compliance. "We are not just negotiators," she told me. "We are guardians of the organization's value chain. However, how can we be strategic when drowning in repetitive tasks?" Her words stuck with me because they reflected the silent frustration of countless leaders, I have met leaders who want to make a difference but are shackled by inefficiencies. Then, an HR head at a technology firm shared their frustration with the volume of employee queries, most of which were repetitive. Their team was stretched thin, leaving little room for initiatives that could elevate employee engagement or foster a stronger company culture.

The legal department of a multinational manufacturing firm once confided how daunting it was to review contracts under tight deadlines. "Each clause we review feels like a ticking time bomb," the general counsel said. "One oversight and we could expose the company to enormous risks. However, with the volume of contracts we handle, it feels inevitable that something will slip through the cracks." And then, there is Finance—a function where precision meets pressure. I remember working with a large organization on a project to overhaul its overhead spend management process. The Finance leader shared how fragmented systems and manual workflows made budgeting, forecasting, and tracking overheads a nightmare. "It is like trying to build a puzzle with half the pieces missing," he said. "The numbers never quite align, and it is too late to act by the time we get clarity. We need something more innovative.

The Bigger Picture

These conversations are not isolated incidents; they reflect many leaders' struggles in their day-to-day operations. Technology promises to be the panacea, but how often does it truly deliver? Over the years, I have noticed that while automation tools and software have made incremental improvements, they have rarely addressed the core challenge: helping leaders move beyond tasks to focus on strategy and innovation.
This is where Generative AI enters the picture, not as another solution in the crowded tech landscape but as a transformative enabler. It is not just about making processes faster; it is about making them more intelligent. A generative AI-based solution does not just process databases understand it. It does not just automate tasks—it augments human decision-making. Imagine a Procurement team no longer combing through contracts line by line but instead receiving a concise summary of risky clauses, supplier dependencies, and ESG compliance issues in minutes. Consider an HR department that can instantly respond to employee queries while analyzing data to identify patterns that predict attrition. Picture a Legal team that can precisely extract key precedents from thousands of case laws or a Finance department that can forecast trends and uncover anomalies before they become problems.

These are not futuristic scenarios; they are happening today and are powered by Generative AI. So, as you read this chapter, do not just think of these use cases as stories about other companies. Think of them as possibilities for your organization. What would your team accomplish if you could eliminate the mundane and focus on the meaningful? What innovations would you unlock if your processes were more innovative, faster, and more adaptive? This chapter will explore specific use cases for each function in detail. Let us start with Procurement, where every penny saved directly contributes to the bottom line.

Transforming Procurement

Procurement has always been a balancing act—managing costs, ensuring compliance, and meeting deadlines while juggling countless supplier interactions. Generative AI uniquely enhances Procurement by autonomously generating content, insights, and adaptive solutions—from contracts to RFPs and supplier evaluations, driving efficiency, accuracy, and innovation. Its transformative role enables autonomous, insight-driven procurement operations.

Over the years, leaders have grappled with an overwhelming volume of low-value, high-frequency purchases, especially in tail spending. Often too small to merit dedicated resources, these transactions create inefficiencies that drain time and energy. It is like trying to climb a mountain while carrying a bag of pebbles—individually light but collectively burdensome. We will keep the focus of this section on autonomous buying, as this is one of the complex use cases and covers many other generative AI scenarios. Autonomous Buying does not just streamline tail spending—it fundamentally redefines how organizations manage Procurement. By automating repetitive, low-value tasks, procurement teams can shift their focus to strategic initiatives like supplier innovation, risk mitigation, and sustainability. It can be a game-changer - Imagine building a digital twin of your procurement team, where every key role—from category managers to supplier analysts—is represented by AI agents working collaboratively. This is not a futuristic pipe dream but a practical solution for automating and optimizing low-value purchases while maintaining governance and strategic alignment.

Take, for example, a global FMCG company overwhelmed by thousands of small, non-strategic purchases annually. Implementing this system could reduce procurement cycle times from weeks to hours, achieve significant cost savings, and ensure compliance with minimal human intervention. This is not about replacing people; it is about empowering them. Imagine category managers freed from mundane tasks, focusing instead on building strategic supplier relationships. Visualize procurement leaders leveraging real-time insights to drive transformative changes. Autonomous Buying powered by Generative AI is not just a technological evolution but a call to reimagine what Procurement can achieve.

Multi-Agent Design for Autonomous Buying

At the heart of Autonomous Buying lies a *multi-agent system* orchestrated by a central AI-powered agent, the "Orchestrator." This Orchestrator is like a symphony conductor, ensuring harmony between various specialized AI agents, each representing a distinct procurement role.

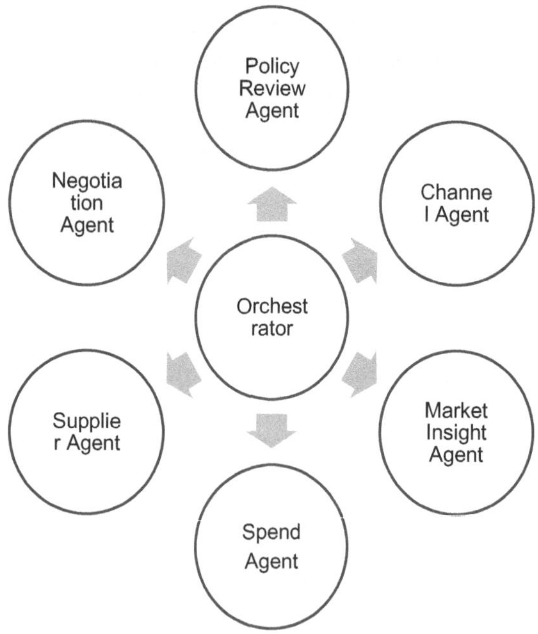

Fig 9.1: Key AI Agent Roles and Responsibilities in Autonomous Buying

This diagram illustrates the various AI agent roles involved in autonomous buying and a visual representation of how different AI agents interact and are coordinated by the Orchestrator Agent in an autonomous buying system. Each agent has a specific role that contributes to the overall efficiency and effectiveness of the buying process. This visual helps understand the distribution of responsibilities and the flow of tasks among the agents, as further explained below.

Key AI Agent Roles and Responsibilities in Autonomous Buying

Orchestrator Agent

Description: The central controller coordinates activities among all other agents, ensuring smooth workflows and timely task assignments.

Responsibilities

- Assign tasks to relevant agents based on the requisition type.
- Aggregate outputs from various agents and finalize decisions.
- Provide real-time updates to the requester.

Example: An employee requests ergonomic office chairs. The **Orchestrator Agent**

receives and assigns the request to the appropriate agents based on predefined workflows.

Channel Agent

Description: Determines if the requisition belongs to a predefined category or is an ad-hoc (non-category) spend.

Responsibilities:

- Map requisition items to predefined categories.
- Route non-mapped items to the relevant agent for further validation.

Example: The Channel Agent identifies the chairs as belonging to the "Office Furniture" category. The request is routed to the **Category service** for further processing.

Policy Agent

Description: Ensures compliance with organizational policies and guidelines.

Responsibilities:

- Validate budget thresholds and approval levels.
- Check adherence to sustainability (ESG) or regional regulations.
- Ensure supplier certifications are up to date.

Example: The Policy Agent confirms that the requested chairs fall within the budget limit for ergonomic equipment and comply with sustainability requirements.

Spend Insight Agent

Description: Reviews past procurement data to identify patterns, trends, and opportunities for cost optimization.

Responsibilities:

- Check for existing contracts with preferred suppliers.
- Suggest bundling opportunities based on historical purchases.

Example: The agent identifies a similar purchase from six months ago with a preferred supplier. It recommends using the same supplier to expedite the process and potentially benefit from loyalty discounts.

Supplier Evaluation Agent

Description: Evaluates and selects the best supplier based on predefined criteria.

Responsibilities:

- Evaluate historical performance metrics (e.g., delivery accuracy, quality).
- Assess compliance with certifications and sustainability requirements.

Example: The agent recommends a supplier with a track record of on-time delivery and a 10% discount for bulk orders. If the requested supplier is not approved, it suggests alternatives that meet organizational standards.

Negotiation Agent

Description: Engages with suppliers to optimize terms, pricing, and delivery timelines.

Responsibilities:

- Use market trends and historical data to negotiate better pricing.
- Optimize delivery timelines for urgent needs.
- Negotiate payment terms (e.g., early payment discounts).

Example: The agent secures a 10% discount by bundling the order with another department's requisition and negotiates faster delivery by leveraging historical order volumes.

Enhancing Autonomous Buying with Human-in-the-Loop

While the multi-agent design in autonomous buying enables remarkable automation and optimization, incorporating **human-in-the-loop (HITL)** ensures excellent reliability, accountability, and adaptability. HITL integrates human expertise at key decision points to oversee, validate, or intervene, when necessary, particularly in complex, high-risk, or edge-case scenarios.

Here is how it works in practice:

Scenario: Purchasing Chairs for a New Office Setup

- **Requisition Submission**: Employee submits a request for 100 ergonomic chairs. The Orchestrator routes the request to relevant agents.
- **Channel Agent Decision**: Classifies the request as category spend.
- **Policy Compliance Review**: The Policy Agent flags the request for exceeding the budget threshold and escalates it for human review.

- **Supplier Selection**: The Supplier Agent identifies two potential suppliers. A human reviews the trade-off between cost and delivery speed.
- **Negotiation**: The Negotiation Agent secures a 10% discount, but a supplier counteroffer involves early payment terms. Human approval is sought to finalize the deal.
- **Approval and Execution**: The Orchestrator consolidates all inputs, including human approvals, and places the order.

Outcome: Chairs are delivered at a 10% discount, with human-approved payment terms and policy compliance ensured.

By integrating HITL into the multi-agent framework, organizations achieve a balance between automation and human expertise. This ensures procurement processes are efficient, reliable, and aligned with organizational priorities while maintaining flexibility for nuanced decision-making.

Transforming HR

Talent acquisition has always been a high-stakes challenge for HR leaders. Finding the perfect fit for a role is not just about filling vacancies, it is about ensuring the proper alignment between a candidate's potential and an organization's culture and goals. However, as I have often heard from HR professionals during digital transformation discussions, this process is riddled with inefficiencies. The volume of applications, the manual review of resumes, and the pressure to craft personalized outreach for high-potential candidates can be overwhelming. One HR leader once shared their frustration: "*We spend hours screening resumes and writing job descriptions, but we still end up missing out on top talent. By the time we identify someone, they have already moved on to another offer.*" This scenario is not unique. In today's competitive job market, where top talent is snapped up within days, HR teams need to move faster without compromising the quality of their decisions. Generative AI can transform talent acquisition by streamlining processes, personalizing engagement, and unlocking insights buried in unstructured data.

Reimagining the Talent Acquisition Process

Crafting Tailored Job Descriptions

A common pain point for HR teams is creating job descriptions that are not only accurate but also appealing. Generative AI can assist by analyzing successful hires from the past and generating customized job descriptions tailored to the target audience.

For instance:

- For a tech role, AI might emphasize growth opportunities and cutting-edge projects.
- For a creative position, it could highlight the company's design culture and flexible work environment.

These descriptions can be fine-tuned further with HR input, ensuring they reflect the role's technical requirements and the company's values.

Intelligent Resume Screening

HR teams often receive hundreds, if not thousands, of applications for a single role. Sifting through these resumes is not only time-consuming but also prone to biases. Generative AI can act as an intelligent screener, analyzing resumes for key skills, experiences, and achievements. However, it does not stop there—it can also process unstructured data within resumes, like project descriptions or personal achievements, to identify unique strengths.

For example:

- A candidate who managed a small team to deliver a project under tight deadlines might be flagged as having leadership potential.
- Another candidate who has worked across industries could be identified as adaptable and resourceful.

Generative AI ensures no promising candidate goes unnoticed, providing HR with a ranked shortlist and detailed insights into why each candidate is a good fit.

Personalized Candidate Outreach

Top talent often requires more than a standard email to pique their interest. Generative AI can analyze a candidate's resume, LinkedIn profile, and publicly available portfolios to craft highly personalized outreach messages.

For example:

- For a candidate with a strong background in sustainability, the AI might generate a message highlighting the company's green initiatives.
- For someone with entrepreneurial experience, it could focus on opportunities to lead new initiatives or innovation projects.

This level of personalization not only improves response rates but also demonstrates that the organization values and understands the candidate's unique qualities.

Analysing Interview Transcripts

Interviews generate much-unstructured data, often captured as notes or recordings. Generative AI can analyze this data to extract insights, such as a candidate's communication style, problem-solving approach, or cultural fit.

For instance:

- A candidate who consistently emphasizes teamwork and collaboration is an excellent fit for cross-functional roles.
- Another who offers innovative solutions during case-study interviews is a potential hire for strategy focused positions.

Talent acquisition is about filling roles and building an organization's future. Generative AI does not replace the human touch in hiring—it amplifies it. By automating repetitive tasks and uncovering insights hidden in unstructured data, HR teams can focus on what truly matters: building meaningful connections with top talent and aligning them with the company's vision.

As an HR leader, ask yourself: *What would it mean for your team if the time spent on manual tasks was reinvested in strategic talent planning? How impactful could your hiring process be if you had a tool that found talent and understood it?*

Generative AI is not just a tool but an enabler, helping HR teams navigate the complexities of modern talent acquisition with intelligence, empathy, and precision.

Transforming Legal

The legal profession has long been a bastion of tradition, where complex processes and intricate details often slow down progress. From my experience in digital transformation, I have worked closely with legal teams and seen firsthand how manual processes, such as contract review and redlining, can drain time and resources. Many legal professionals know it is a challenge: navigating endless rounds of document revisions, catching minor errors, and managing the constant back-and-forth between parties—all while trying to ensure compliance, mitigate risks, and maintain efficiency.

Generative AI, when applied to **legal redlining**, can potentially revolutionize legal teams' operations.

The Challenge with Traditional Redlining

Legal redlining, reviewing, revising, and negotiating contracts—can be time-consuming and prone to human error. Whether reviewing a vendor agreement, a partnership contract, or an M&A document, lawyers must manually markup contracts, track changes, and ensure all clauses comply with legal standards. The back-and-forth process between legal teams, vendors, and partners adds complexity.

Over the years, I have witnessed this firsthand in client projects, where legal departments could spend hours, if not days, drafting, reviewing, and redlining contracts, only to find discrepancies or critical clauses overlooked after finalizing the document. The challenge is not just the volume of contracts but also the need for accuracy in each revision—errors can be costly financially and reputationally.

Generative AI for Legal Redlining

Generative AI transforms this labor-intensive, error-prone task into a seamless, innovative workflow. By embedding AI into the legal redlining process, organizations can reduce manual effort and ensure that each contract revision is precise, compliant, and aligned with company standards.

Let us walk through how Generative AI can be applied in this context:

- Automated Clause Detection:The first step is contract analysis. Traditionally, a legal professional read through the document to identify key clauses, terms, and potential risks. With Generative AI, the system can instantly identify and categorize the clauses in a contract, such as indemnity clauses, payment terms, liability limitations, and intellectual property provisions. AI algorithms, trained on historical contract data, can identify patterns and flag any clause that deviates from typical contract language or might pose a potential risk.

Example: Imagine a legal team reviewing a partnership agreement. The AI agent scans the document and flags a clause related to payment terms, not in line with the company's usual agreement, suggesting an alternative based on previous contracts. This reduces the time spent on manual review and ensures consistency across all agreements.

- Real-Time Redlining Suggestions: Once clauses are identified, Generative AI can make real-time recommendations for revisions. This is not just about detecting errors; the AI understands the context and nuances of the contract and can propose changes that align with company policies or best legal practices. For example, if a clause seems overly favorable to the supplier and might expose the company to unnecessary risk, AI can suggest more balanced language based on past negotiations.

Example: A supplier agreement includes a clause allowing unlimited price increases over the contract term. The AI agent flags this and suggests an alternative clause based on historical contracts that limit price increases to a fixed percentage, mitigating potential financial risks.

- Automated Compliance Checks: One of the most crucial aspects of legal redlining is ensuring compliance with internal company policies and external regulations. Generative AI can be programmed to automatically cross-check contract clauses with relevant regulatory frameworks, compliance guidelines, and company standards.

Example: In a contract for a global partnership, the AI checks for GDPR compliance in the data protection clauses, ensuring that the language is aligned with the most recent privacy laws. It flags non-compliant clauses and suggests edits aligning the document with regulations.

- Risk Mitigation and Smart Recommendations: Beyond just identifying issues, Generative AI can assess potential risks based on historical data and external sources like case law or industry news. If a contract includes a clause that's been the subject of litigation or has caused problems in the past, the AI can flag this and propose alternative, risk-reducing language.

Example: Imagine a legal team reviewing a contract for a merger, and the AI flags a particular clause in the indemnity section that has historically led to litigation. Based on similar cases, AI suggests changes to mitigate this risk, offering a more balanced approach to indemnification.

The Impact of Generative AI on Legal Teams

For legal professionals, the ability to automate redlining with Generative AI has a profound impact. It accelerates the entire contract lifecycle, reduces errors, and ensures consistency across all legal agreements. However, beyond efficiency, it frees legal teams to focus on higher-value activities, such as strategy, risk analysis, and complex negotiations. Consider a global organization with hundreds of contracts across various departments. With Generative AI in place, their legal teams can process these contracts faster, more accurately, and with fewer resources, allowing them to allocate time and effort to strategic legal issues that drive business growth. As you reflect on these possibilities, think about your organization. Could AI-powered redlining streamline your legal processes, freeing your team to focus on high-impact work? What risks could be mitigated with more innovative, faster contract management? Generative AI is not just transforming legal departments—it is helping them unlock new possibilities for efficiency, accuracy, and strategic growth.

Transforming Finance

In the fast-paced world of Finance, every decision counts. Finance leaders are constantly pressured to provide timely insights, manage risk, optimize performance, and communicate effectively with stakeholders. Finance professionals are often stuck in a cycle of producing reports, tracking performance, and dealing with complex spreadsheets—essential tasks but leave little time for strategic decision-making or forward-thinking. The traditional finance workflow, though effective, tends to focus on compliance and historical data, leaving the future largely uncharted. Generative AI has the potential to break the shackles of manual data entry and static reporting, allowing finance professionals to focus on strategy, forecasting, and value-driven insights.

AI-Generated Financial

Narratives

Imagine this: It is the end of the quarter, and your finance team is deep in the weeds, trying to put together a comprehensive financial report for senior leadership. They have compiled all the numbers, reconciled accounts, and reviewed key performance indicators. However, one crucial piece remains—the narrative. How do you translate dry numbers into a story that explains the company's financial health? What does a 5% increase in operational costs mean for your long-term strategy?

This is where Generative AI shines. Powered by large language models, Generative AI can automatically generate detailed financial narratives, summarizing key financial metrics and translating them into actionable insights. Instead of spending hours drafting text, your team could feed the numbers and let the AI generate a well-written, insightful summary that highlights important trends, anomalies, and opportunities.

For example, imagine an AI that produces a quarterly financial report with the following:

- Revenue Growth Analysis: "This quarter saw a 10% increase in revenue, driven primarily by growth in the North American market. The adoption of our new product line contributed 4% to the overall increase, surpassing initial forecasts."
- Expense Breakdown: "Expenses increased by 5%, largely due to higher raw material costs in the manufacturing process. However, cost-saving measures in logistics reduced overall shipping expenses by 2%."

This AI-generated narrative saves your team hours of manual work, allowing them to focus on deeper analysis rather than writing reports. Moreover, AI does not just generate text—it contextualizes the numbers within the broader business environment, helping leaders quickly grasp the company's financial health.

Mergers & Acquisitions (M&A) Analysis

Mergers and acquisitions (M&A) are complex processes that involve significant financial analysis and risk assessments. Traditionally, finance teams analyze financial statements, legal documents, market data, and other key metrics to evaluate the viability of a merger or acquisition. However, this process can be slow, prone to oversight, and often lacks the agility required in a fast-moving market.

Generative AI can streamline M&A analysis by rapidly processing vast amounts of data from multiple sources, such as financial reports, market conditions, and news articles. AI models can generate detailed insights, simulate potential outcomes, and assess the strategic alignment between two companies, all of which can aid in making better-informed decisions.

Example: A multinational corporation is considering acquiring a smaller competitor. Instead of manually analyzing years of financial statements, legal documents, and market reports, the finance team uses Generative AI to summarize key data points, identify potential synergies, and forecast post-acquisition financial outcomes. Gen AI also compares the two companies' strategic goals and suggests possible challenges in integration. This drastically reduces the time spent on due diligence and allows the leadership team to make quicker, more informed decisions.

Automating Compliance and Regulatory Reporting

Compliance with financial regulations is an ongoing challenge for organizations of all sizes. It requires careful attention to detail and timely reporting, whether adhering to tax laws, monitoring financial transactions for money laundering, or staying up to date with changing global regulations. Staying compliant can become a monumental task with the increasing complexity of financial regulations. Generative AI can help automate compliance by processing complex regulatory frameworks, continuously monitoring financial operations, and generating reports that ensure adherence to local and global laws. AI can also track regulation changes and automatically update compliance protocols, ensuring the finance team always works with the most current information.

Example: A multinational financial services company must file quarterly reports that comply with multiple regulatory standards across various countries. By leveraging Generative AI, the company can automatically generate compliance reports covering all necessary regulations, ensuring they meet the required standards in each jurisdiction. Furthermore, the AI can monitor regulatory updates and adapt the company's financial practices as new laws come into effect, significantly reducing the manual effort needed and minimizing the risk of non-compliance. Generative AI is reshaping the way finance departments operate. It is not just about speeding up reporting or automating routine tasks but about creating new possibilities for innovation, efficiency, and strategic decision-making. Whether it is generating insightful financial narratives, gathering market intelligence, or automating regulatory compliance, the potential of Generative AI to transform Finance is immense.

Conclusion

In this chapter, we have explored the transformative potential of Generative AI across key horizontal business functions: Procurement, HR, Legal, and Finance. By delving into specific use cases, we have seen how Generative AI can drive efficiency, accuracy, and innovation, fundamentally altering how organizations operate.For Procurement, Autonomous Buying redefines how low-value, high-frequency purchases are managed, allowing teams to focus on strategic initiatives. In HR, Generative AI streamlines talent acquisition processes, from crafting job descriptions to personalized candidate outreach, ensuring no potential talent is overlooked. Legal departments can leverage AI for automated clause detection, real-time redlining suggestions, and compliance checks, significantly reducing the time and effort spent on contract management. Finally, AI-generated narratives, M&A analysis, and automated compliance reporting in Finance free finance professionals from manual tasks, enabling them to focus on strategic decision-making and value-driven insights.

Generative AI is not merely an automation tool but an enabler of more innovative, faster, and more adaptive business processes. It allows leaders to move beyond mundane tasks and focus on what truly matters—strategic planning, innovation, and growth. Considering the possibilities discussed in this chapter, envision how these AI-driven solutions could transform your organization, unlocking new levels of efficiency and strategic capability. The future of business operations is not just about doing things faster; it is about doing them smarter.

Exercise: Test Your Understanding

Answer the following questions and test your understanding of learning from

Chapter 9:

Q. 1. What are the primary business functions discussed in the chapter where Generative AI can be applied?

Q. 2. How does Generative AI enhance the Procurement process, particularly in autonomous buying?

Q. 3. In the context of HR, how can Generative AI improve the talent acquisition process?

Q. 4. What are the key benefits of applying Generative AI in Legal departments for contract management?

Q. 5. How can Generative AI transform financial reporting and compliance in Finance?

10

Leveraging Generative AI for Industry Verticals

The transformative power of Generative AI is no longer confined to horizontal functions like HR or finance; instead, it is reshaping the way industries operate, innovate, and deliver value. As someone who has architected solutions across diverse verticals, I have observed firsthand how Generative AI addresses specific pain points in Manufacturing, Automobile/Mobility, and Finance—industries traditionally resistant to rapid change due to legacy systems, stringent regulations, and operational complexities. Each industry has distinct challenges and opportunities that require tailored AI solutions. In Manufacturing, the need for process optimization and predictive maintenance aligns naturally with Generative AI's capabilities in data synthesis and anomaly detection. For Automobiles and Mobility, AI accelerates innovation, from autonomous systems to personalized customer experiences. Finance, perhaps the most tightly regulated industry, embraces Generative AI for fraud detection, risk management, and customer personalization. This chapter aims to delve into these unique applications, illustrating how Generative AI drives efficiency, reduces costs, and unlocks new business opportunities. By the end of this chapter, you will gain actionable insights into leveraging AI within their industries.

Addressing Industry-Specific Challenges

Generative AI's strength lies in its ability to process and analyze vast amounts of structured and unstructured data, create meaningful insights, and generate innovative solutions that align with industry-specific requirements.

However, each industry presents unique challenges that demand customized approaches:

- **Manufacturing** is characterized by intricate supply chains, high-stakes production lines, and the need for precision and efficiency. Legacy systems, still prevalent in this sector, often struggle to integrate modern technologies, leaving manufacturers relying on outdated methods for decision-making. Generative AI bridges this gap by optimizing production processes, analyzing equipment failures, and driving innovation in product design.

- **Automobile and mobility** industries are disrupting, with electrification, autonomous driving, and shared mobility services fundamentally reshaping business models. These industries require advanced solutions to accelerate R&D, enhance customer experiences, and optimize fleet management. Generative AI enables breakthroughs in autonomous systems, vehicle performance analytics, and personalized user interfaces.
- **Finance and** banking are some of the most tightly regulated sectors, and trust and accuracy are paramount. Challenges such as fraud, compliance, risk assessment, and customer personalization demand robust and adaptive solutions. Generative AI is stepping up to deliver on these fronts by improving risk modeling and providing tailored financial advice to clients.

Let us begin with the **Manufacturing** industry, where Generative AI has been instrumental in driving the next wave of industrial revolution.

Generative AI Use Cases in Manufacturing

Manufacturing is an industry of complexity—multiple suppliers, intricate production processes, and ever-increasing quality standards. Generative AI is emerging as a catalyst for transformation, addressing these complexities through intelligent automation, optimization, and innovation. Let us explore how Generative AI redefines Manufacturing with practical, real-world applications.

Product Design and Prototyping: Redefining Innovation

Innovation has always been the lifeblood of Manufacturing. From the first assembly lines to the advent of lean Manufacturing, every leap forward has been powered by the ability to turn ideas into tangible, functional products. However, today, as markets grow more competitive and customer expectations soar, the pace of innovation must accelerate like never before. Traditional design processes often involve significant manual effort. Engineers draft blueprints, refine them based on feedback, and iterate endlessly to find the right balance between form, function, and cost. Generative AI, however, flips this model on its head by generating multiple design options based on predefined parameters, allowing teams to focus on evaluating rather than creating from scratch.

Imagine an automotive company tasked with designing a new chassis for electric vehicles. The goals are clear: It must be lightweight to maximize battery efficiency, durable to withstand wear and tear, and cost-effective for mass production. By inputting these constraints into a Generative AI model—parameters like weight limits, material strength, and budgetary constraints—the team can instantly receive dozens, even hundreds, of design variations.

One AI-generated design might suggest using a honeycomb structure made of composite materials to balance strength and weight. Another could propose an innovative tubular design that reduces manufacturing costs. The AI does not just present ideas—it backs them with data, showing how each design performs under simulated stress tests or in virtual wind tunnels.

Supply Chain Optimization: Navigating Complexity with Precision

The supply chain is the lifeline of modern businesses—a vast, interconnected system that requires seamless coordination of resources, processes, and data. As organizations strive to remain competitive in increasingly dynamic markets, they face challenges like fluctuating demand, unpredictable disruptions, and escalating costs. **Generative AI** emerges as a transformative solution, offering the ability to optimize supply chain operations with unmatched precision and adaptability.

Emerging Models: Time Series Transformers for Enhanced Forecasting

Generative AI is advancing beyond traditional machine learning, now incorporating time series transformers designed to predict sequential numerical data. Much like large language models (such as GPT) anticipate the next word in a sentence, these transformers specialize in forecasting the next value in a time series.

Unlike traditional forecasting models, time series transformers can handle complex, multi-variable datasets with irregular intervals. Their adaptability makes them ideal for modern supply chain challenges where variables like demand, pricing, and lead times are interdependent.

Demand Forecasting: Anticipating Market Needs

Accurate demand forecasting is the cornerstone of an efficient supply chain. Overestimating demand leads to overproduction, increased inventory costs, and waste, while underestimating it results in stockouts and lost revenue. Generative AI time series transformer models can address these challenges by analyzing multiple data sources.

Training and Knowledge Sharing: Building a Skilled Workforce with Manufacturing Copilot

In a world where manufacturing processes grow more complex by the day, the role of a well-trained workforce is critical. However, traditional training methods often fall short in keeping pace with the rapid technological advancements and the increasing demands of precision, safety, and efficiency. This is where a Manufacturing Copilot powered by Generative AI becomes a game-changer. By acting as a dynamic knowledge hub and real-time mentor, the Copilot ensures that every employee, from novices to seasoned experts, has the tools and information they need to succeed.

Generative AI in the Automotive \ Mobile Sector

To understand how generative AI is poised to revolutionize the automotive and mobility sector, it is first essential to grasp this industry's complexity and dynamism. Over the past century, the automotive world has evolved from a symbol of industrial innovation to a sophisticated ecosystem where engineering brilliance meets digital ingenuity. Today, vehicles are no longer just machines that transport people from one place to another—they are platforms for connectivity, sustainability, and personalized experiences. Electric vehicles (EVs) are reshaping perceptions of environmental responsibility, while autonomous driving redefines the concept of mobility.

Meanwhile, the rise of connected cars and mobility-as-a-service (MaaS) solutions hints at a future where ownership takes a back seat to shared convenience.

However, beneath the surface of these transformative trends lies a landscape rife with challenges. The pressure to innovate is immense as automakers race to develop electric drivetrains, advanced driver-assistance systems (ADAS), and autonomous technologies that are both cutting-edge, safe, reliable, and cost-effective. This innovation must occur within a highly fragmented regulatory environment, where emissions standards, safety requirements, and data privacy laws vary drastically across regions. Moreover, global supply chains strained by recent disruptions such as semiconductor shortages must adapt to the growing demand for high-tech components and sustainable materials.

At the same time, the automotive customer has become more discerning than ever. They expect vehicles that are functional and tailored to their unique needs, complete with personalized interiors, seamless digital interfaces, and eco-friendly credentials. Meeting these expectations is no small feat, especially as manufacturers grapple with transitioning to software-centric vehicles. Software now defines the modern driving experience, powering everything from infotainment to over-the-air updates and predictive maintenance. For legacy automakers, this shift demands a complete reimagining of their design and production processes.

Adding to these pressures is the growing urgency around sustainability. Beyond the production of EVs, the industry faces scrutiny over its carbon footprint throughout the entire vehicle lifecycle, from manufacturing to recycling. Urbanization introduces another layer of complexity, with increasing congestion, parking shortages, and pollution forcing companies to innovate beyond traditional vehicles to address the unique challenges of densely populated cities.

As the industry teeters between disruption and reinvention, generative AI stands as a catalyst for innovation, promising solutions that could redefine how we design, manufacture, and experience mobility in the years to come

Below are several impactful use cases where Generative AI can drive innovation:

In-Vehicle Assistant

Generative AI is revolutionizing how users interact with their vehicles, transforming them from mere modes of transportation into intelligent companions. Advanced in-vehicle assistants, powered by natural language understanding and real-time data processing, are at the heart of this transformation. These assistants redefine convenience and safety, making every drive more innovative and enjoyable.

One of the most significant advancements is personalized navigation. By considering user preferences—such as avoiding toll roads, scenic route preferences, or the availability of electric vehicle (EV) charging stations—alongside real-time traffic conditions, these AI-driven systems provide optimal routes tailored to individual needs. Imagine an EV driver seamlessly guided to a fast-charging station, perfectly timed with their journey's demands. This level of personalization not only reduces stress but also enhances efficiency. In-vehicle assistants also shine in voice interaction. Gone are the days of clunky, rigid commands; today's systems understand conversational language, enabling drivers to adjust climate controls, change music playlists, or even activate safety features with effortless natural speech. Whether asking for weather updates or requesting specific seat settings, the interaction feels intuitive and human-like, minimizing driver distraction. Safety is another domain in which these assistants excel. Through proactive safety recommendations, they can monitor factors like driver fatigue, road conditions, and weather forecasts, offering timely alerts. For instance, a gentle reminder to take a break after prolonged driving or cautionary advice about icy roads ahead can significantly improve on-road safety, turning the assistant into a guardian as much as a guide

Smart Dealership Support

Generative AI extends its transformative reach beyond the vehicle, enhancing the dealership experience for customers and staff. AI-driven solutions streamline and make the traditionally time-intensive and often overwhelming process of purchasing or servicing a vehicle more engaging. A **virtual sales assistant** powered by generative AI is an informed, always-available guide for prospective buyers. This assistant can walk customers through a vehicle's features, suggest configurations based on their needs, and even explain financing options with unparalleled clarity. For instance, a family-oriented buyer might receive recommendations emphasizing safety features and cargo space, while an urban commuter might be introduced to compact, fuel-efficient models. This personalized approach fosters trust and satisfaction.

Customer Experience Personalization

Generative AI is a game-changer in delivering personalized customer experiences, enabling automakers to forge deeper connections with their users. By analyzing customer data, AI can anticipate preferences, enhance interactions, and make ownership more enjoyable.

Personalized marketing is one of the most visible benefits. Automakers can craft bespoke offers based on a customer's driving habits, purchase history, and lifestyle choices. An EV owner who frequently drives long distances might receive tailored promotions for high-capacity charging accessories, while a city driver might be offered incentives on compact, urban-friendly vehicles. This level of specificity not only boosts engagement but also enhances customer loyalty.

AI-driven support further enriches the customer's experience by providing instant, accurate query responses. Whether a driver needs help troubleshooting a dashboard warning light or wants guidance on optimizing fuel efficiency, the AI assistant offers precise solutions in real time. Its ability to handle many questions ensures no customer is left waiting for help.

Generative AI also unlocks **ownership insights** that add value throughout the vehicle lifecycle. It can analyze a user's driving habits to suggest optimal vehicle settings or recommend accessories that enhance functionality. For example, an AI assistant might notice frequent off-road trips and propose all-weather floor mats or vehicle protection packages tailored for rugged use. It could also remind drivers about service plans aligned with their usage patterns, ensuring the vehicle remains in peak condition.

Generative AI in Financial Service

The financial services sector operates in a fast-paced, highly regulated environment where customer expectations for personalized, efficient, and seamless experiences are ever-growing. Generative AI is emerging as a transformative force, enabling institutions to reimagine traditional processes, enhance customer interactions, and drive operational efficiency. Below are some of the most impactful use cases for generative AI in financial services.

Contact Centre Transformation: Revolutionizing Customer Interactions

Generative AI redefines the customer experience in contact centers by delivering more innovative, faster, and more empathetic interactions. AI-powered virtual agents can handle various customer queries, from account balance checks to complex financial advice, using natural language understanding to ensure the conversation feels human and engaging. These systems can resolve routine inquiries instantly while seamlessly escalating more complex cases to human agents with complete context, reducing wait times and enhancing satisfaction.

Moreover, AI-driven sentiment analysis enables proactive support by gauging customer emotions during interactions. If frustration is detected, the system can guide agents to adopt a more empathetic tone or escalate the matter to a supervisor, ensuring the customer feels valued and understood. This level of personalization strengthens customer relationships and optimizes agent workloads, allowing them to focus on high-value tasks.

Knowledge Search: Accelerating Access to Information

In financial services, timely and accurate access to information is critical. Generative AI empowers employees and customers alike with advanced **knowledge search** capabilities. By indexing vast repositories of documents, policies, and regulatory guidelines, AI can surface precise answers to specific questions in seconds.

For example, a compliance officer could quickly retrieve relevant clauses from regulatory documents, or a customer could effortlessly find details about loan terms without shifting through dense FAQs. This technology eliminates information bottlenecks, enhances decision-making, and reduces the risk of human error, making it an invaluable tool for both front-office and back-office operations.

Wealth Advisor Training and Simulation: Preparing Advisors for Real-World Challenges

Training wealth advisors often requires significant time and resources, but generative AI offers a transformative approach through realistic simulations and tailored learning experiences. AI can create interactive scenarios where advisors practice responding to complex client inquiries or market shifts, receiving instant feedback to hone their skills.

For example, a trainee might engage in a simulated discussion with an AI-powered client avatar seeking advice on diversifying their portfolio. The AI evaluates the advisor's responses, offering suggestions for improvement and highlighting areas for further study. This method accelerates learning and ensures advisors are well-prepared for high-stakes interactions.

Know Your Product (KYP): Simplifying Complex Offerings

Financial products are often intricate, with terms, features, and risks that can overwhelm customers and employees. Generative AI simplifies this complexity through tools that dynamically explain product details in clear, concise language tailored to the user's level of understanding.

For example, a bank offering a structured investment product can use AI to generate personalized explanations, breaking down key features, risks, and benefits in a way that resonates with each customer. This ensures transparency, reduces confusion, and builds trust.

PitchBook Generation: Automating High-Impact Presentations

Creating pitch books for investment opportunities or client presentations is a resource-intensive task that requires significant research and design. Generative AI automates this process by generating professional, data-driven pitch books incorporating client-specific data, market trends, and visualizations.

For example, an investment banker preparing a pitch for a merger can use AI to draft a polished presentation complete with financial projections, industry benchmarks, and risk analyses, allowing the team to focus on strategy rather than formatting.

Conclusion

As we conclude this chapter, Generative AI is a powerful catalyst for change across various industry verticals. Its ability to synthesize and analyze data, generate innovative solutions, and adapt to specific industry requirements makes it indispensable for organizations seeking to stay competitive in an increasingly complex and dynamic market. By optimizing production processes, enhancing product design, and streamlining supply chains, Generative AI revolutionizes manufacturing efficiency and innovation. In the Automobile/Mobility sector, AI-driven in-vehicle assistants and personalized experiences redefine customer interactions and vehicle design. In Finance, AI addresses critical challenges like fraud detection and risk management while enhancing customer personalization and operational efficiency. Embracing Generative AI is essential for organizations to stay competitive and drive business transformation, paving the way for the next industrial revolution.

As we move forward, the continued integration of Generative AI into industry-specific applications will undoubtedly lead to even more groundbreaking advancements, reshaping the landscape of Manufacturing, mobility, finance, and beyond. The journey of leveraging Generative AI is just beginning, and those who pioneer its adoption will be at the forefront of the next industrial revolution.

Exercise: Test Your Understanding

Answer the following questions and test your understanding of learning from

`Chapter 10`:

`Q. 1.` How is Generative AI transforming the manufacturing industry?

`Q. 2.` What are some specific use cases of Generative AI in the automobile and mobility sectors?

`Q. 3.` How does Generative AI address challenges in the financial services industry?

`Q. 4.` What is the role of Generative AI in product design and prototyping within Manufacturing?

`Q. 5.` How does Generative AI enhance customer experience personalization in the automotive industry?

11

Responsible AI

AI has become a double-edged sword. On one hand, it offers unprecedented opportunities for innovation, efficiency, and problem-solving. Conversely, when developed or deployed irresponsibly, it can amplify existing inequalities, compromise privacy, and even endanger lives.

Imagine a hiring algorithm that unfairly excludes women or minority candidates due to biased historical data. Alternatively, consider a generative AI system that spreads disinformation at an alarming rate, destabilizing communities. These are not hypothetical scenarios, highlighting the need for urgent action.

AI systems are like mirrors reflecting the data and decisions that shape them. When crafted with care, they amplify human ingenuity and solve pressing problems. However, when built irresponsibly, they magnify biases, exacerbate inequalities, and create new threats. To understand the importance of Responsible AI, we must first examine the consequences of its absence.

Key Implication

Responsible AI embeds Fairness, accountability, and transparency principles into every stage of AI development and deployment. It is about designing technically robust, socially and ethically sound systems.

Amplification of Bias: Learn from AI systems data

If that data contains societal, historical, or systemic biases, the AI will reflect and amplify them

- **Example**: A hiring algorithm designed to screen job applicants excluded women for technical roles because it was trained on historical data where men dominated the field—this perpetuated gender inequality in hiring practices.

- **Example**: A facial recognition system struggled to identify people with darker skin tones because its training data primarily consisted of lighter-skinned individuals, leading to false identifications and wrongful accusations.

Privacy Violations

The more powerful an AI system, the more data it requires. Without safeguards, AI can expose sensitive personal information.

- **Example**: A fitness app shared user location data, inadvertently exposing the locations of military bases when soldiers used the app during exercise.
- **Example**: Smart home devices have been caught recording conversations without consent, raising concerns about surveillance and misuse of private data.

Misinformation and Manipulation

Generative AI, capable of creating highly realistic content, has introduced new challenges in distinguishing fact from fiction.

- **Example**: Deepfake videos have been used to impersonate political figures, spreading misinformation and damaging public trust.
- **Example**: Fake AI-generated reviews on e-commerce platforms mislead consumers, undermining trust in online marketplaces.

Lack of Accountability

When AI systems make mistakes, it is often unclear who is responsible. This lack of accountability can have serious consequences.

- **Example**: In 2018, an autonomous vehicle struck and killed a pedestrian. The tragedy raised questions about liability: Was the fault with the developer, the operator, or the AI itself?

Erosion of Trust in Technology

People who perceive AI as opaque, biased, or unsafe may resist its adoption, even when it could genuinely improve lives.

- **Example**: Public backlash against AI-driven content moderation on social media platforms stemmed from concerns about bias and censorship.

Responsible AI provides a roadmap to avoid these pitfalls. It ensures that AI systems are designed with ethical considerations, societal values, and long-term sustainability.

Core Principles of Responsible AI

The core principles of Responsible AI serve as foundational guidelines to ensure that AI technologies are developed and deployed ethically and responsibly. These principles encompass Fairness, ensuring that AI systems treat all users equitably; Reliability and safety, guaranteeing consistent and safe performance; Privacy and security, protecting user data from misuse and unauthorized access; Inclusiveness, accommodating diverse user needs; Transparency, making AI processes understandable and accountable; and Accountability, holding developers and organizations responsible for AI outcomes. These principles aim to build trust, promote equitable benefits, and minimize potential harms associated with AI applications.

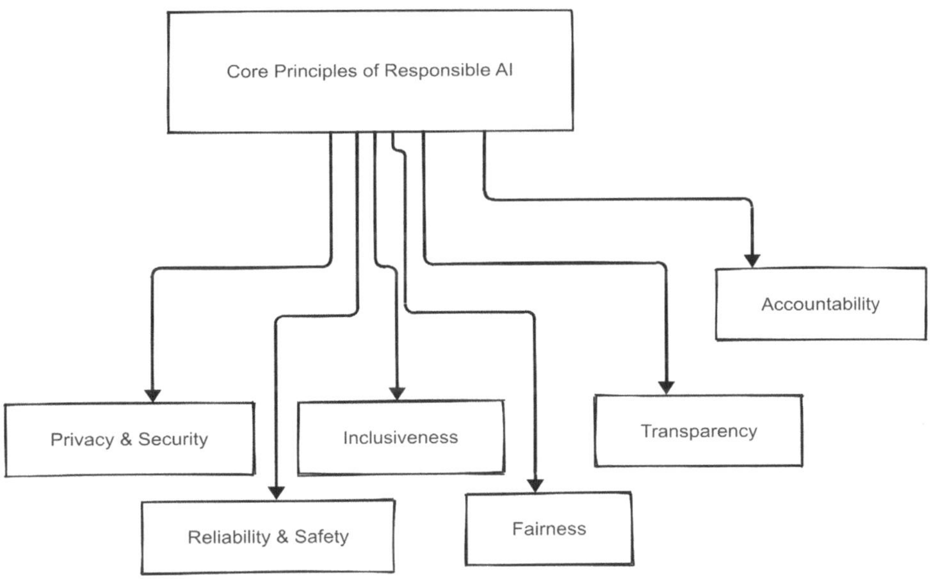

Fig 11.1: Responsible AI

This image illustrates the core principles of Responsible AI, including Fairness, Reliability and safety, Privacy and security, Inclusiveness, Transparency, and Accountability. Each principle is interconnected to ensure that AI technologies are developed and used ethically, reliably, and inclusively.

Fairness

Fairness in AI refers to designing and deploying systems that treat all individuals and groups equitably, avoiding biases that could lead to discriminatory outcomes. AI should not perpetuate existing societal prejudices or amplify inequities in its training data. Fairness ensures that every user—regardless of race, gender, socioeconomic background, or other characteristics—can benefit from the AI system.

Why Fairness Matters

- **Social Impact**: Biased AI systems can exacerbate systemic inequalities, reinforcing stereotypes or excluding marginalized groups.
- **Legal Ramifications**: Discriminatory AI outputs may violate anti-discrimination laws, exposing organizations to lawsuits and reputational damage.
- **Trust and Adoption**: Users are likelier to adopt AI systems they perceive as fair and unbiased, which is critical for long-term success.

Examples of Fairness Challenges in AI

- **Hiring Algorithms**:
    - Problem: A hiring AI trained on historical data showed a preference for male candidates for leadership roles because previous hires were predominantly men.
    - Impact: Qualified female candidates were overlooked, perpetuating gender inequality in the workplace.
    - Fairness Solution: The algorithm could be retrained with balanced datasets or fairness constraints to prevent gender-based discrimination.
- **Loan Approval Systems**:
    - Problem: AI models denied loan applications from certain minority groups because they used proxies like zip codes, which correlated with racial demographics, as part of the decision-making process.
    - Impact: This led to financial exclusion and widened wealth gaps for underrepresented communities.
    - Fairness Solution: Removing biased proxies and ensuring fairness-aware modeling can mitigate these harms.
- **Healthcare Diagnostics**:
    - Problem: AI systems predicting health risks performed less accurately for Black patients because training datasets primarily consisted of data from white populations.
    - Impact: This led to misdiagnoses and unequal access to quality healthcare.
    - Fairness Solution: Collecting diverse datasets and validating AI performance across demographic groups ensures equitable healthcare

delivery

How to Embed Fairness in AI

- **Bias Identification**:
    - Audit datasets for historical or systemic biases.
    - Analyze whether model predictions are equitable across different demographic groups.
- **Inclusive Data Collection**:
    - Ensure training datasets represent diverse populations.
    - Avoid over-representation or under-representation of specific groups.
- **Fairness-Aware Algorithms**:
    - Implement algorithms designed to reduce bias, such as those incorporating fairness constraints.
    - Use techniques like adversarial debiasing or reweighting data to counteract imbalances.
- **Continuous Monitoring**:
    - Regularly evaluate AI outputs to identify and address any emerging biases.
    - To review fairness metrics, involve interdisciplinary teams, including ethicists and domain experts.

Reliability & Safety

Reliability in AI refers to the ability of a system to function consistently, predictably, and accurately under various conditions and across diverse use cases. Safety ensures that these systems do not produce harmful or unintended outcomes, whether physical, psychological, or societal. These principles safeguard trust and usability, especially in high-stakes applications like healthcare, transportation, and financial systems.

Why Reliability & Safety Matter

- **Consistency Across Use Cases**:

- An unreliable AI system may perform excellently in one context but fail in another, leading to errors or harm.
    - Example: A self-driving car must accurately identify pedestrians, traffic lights, and road signs in all weather conditions, whether sunny, rainy, or foggy.
- **Minimizing Harm**:
- AI systems without safety mechanisms can inadvertently cause physical harm, financial loss, or emotional distress.

    - Example: An AI medical diagnostic tool must ensure accurate predictions to avoid misdiagnoses, which could lead to harmful treatments.
- **Building User Trust**:
- Users who perceive AI systems as unreliable or unsafe will resist adoption—even if the system offers significant benefits.
    - Example: Early failures of autonomous vehicles led to skepticism about their safety, delaying public acceptance.

Examples of Reliability & Safety Challenges

- **Autonomous Vehicles**:
    - Problem: A self-driving car failed to recognize a jaywalking pedestrian because its training data only included crosswalk scenarios.
    - Impact: This oversight led to a fatal accident, raising concerns about the safety of autonomous systems.
    - Solution: Comprehensive testing with diverse datasets representing real-world edge cases enhances reliability and safety.
- **Predictive Policing Tools**:
    - Problem: AI tools predicting crime hotspots disproportionately flag low-income neighborhoods due to biased training data.
    - Impact: This reinforced over-policing in certain areas, creating societal harm.
    - Solution: Ensure the system undergoes fairness and safety evaluations, prioritizing societal well-being over predictive accuracy.
- **AI in Finance**:
    - Problem: A stock trading AI made erratic trades during a market downturn due to poorly implemented fail-safe mechanisms.
    - Impact: The company suffered significant financial losses, and investors lost confidence in the system.
    - Solution: Implementing safeguards like stop-loss mechanisms or human override options can mitigate such risks.

How to Embed Reliability & Safety in AI

- **Rigorous Testing Across Scenarios**:
    - Test AI systems under diverse and extreme conditions to ensure robustness.
    - Example: An AI for disaster response should be tested in scenarios involving floods, earthquakes, and other emergencies.
- **Fail-Safe Mechanisms**:
    - Incorporate mechanisms that halt operations when the AI encounters uncertainty or anomalies.

    - Example: Autonomous drones used for delivery should return to a safe base if they lose communication with the control center.
- **Human-in-the-Loop Systems**:
    - Enable human oversight in high-stakes applications to ensure critical decisions are not solely left to AI.
    - Example: In medical diagnostics, AI recommendations should complement, not replace, expert opinions.
- **Continuous Monitoring and Updating**:
    - Regularly monitor the AI's performance and update its algorithms as new data becomes available or conditions evolve.
    - Example: A weather prediction AI must adapt to changing climate patterns to remain accurate.

Reliability and safety are non-negotiable, especially in sectors where errors can have life-threatening or far-reaching consequences. By embedding these principles into the development lifecycle, organizations can ensure that AI systems consistently deliver accurate and harm-free results, earning trust and driving widespread adoption.

Privacy & Security

Privacy refers to protecting user data and ensuring that personal information is not exploited, shared, or misused without consent. Security involves safeguarding AI systems and the data they use from unauthorized access, tampering, and cyberattacks. Privacy and security are the bedrock of trust in AI systems, ensuring users feel confident that their data and interactions are safe.

Why Privacy & Security Matter

- **Protection of Sensitive Data**: AI systems often handle highly personal data, such as health records, financial details, and location information. Mismanagement of this data can result in identity theft, fraud, or loss of privacy.
    - Example: A health monitoring app that exposes user data could lead to unauthorized parties accessing medical histories.
- **Compliance with Regulations**: Governments worldwide have introduced laws like GDPR (General Data Protection Regulation) and CCPA (California Consumer Privacy Act) to enforce data protection. AI systems must align with these regulations to avoid legal penalties.
    - Example: A retail company using AI to analyze customer data must ensure compliance with GDPR to avoid hefty fines.

- **Mitigating Cyber Threats**: AI systems are prime targets for hackers due to the sensitive data they process and the decisions they influence. Ensuring robust security measures prevents breaches and malicious use.
    - Example: Hackers exploiting vulnerabilities in facial recognition systems could bypass security in critical infrastructures like airports.
- **Building Trust**: Users are more likely to adopt AI solutions when they trust that their data is handled securely and ethically.
    - Example: Secure payment gateways using AI fraud detection build trust by safeguarding financial transactions.

Examples of Privacy & Security Challenges

- **Data Leakage**
    - Problem: A fitness tracking AI app accidentally exposed millions of user locations and activity data due to weak encryption.
    - Impact: This raised privacy concerns, putting users at risk of stalking or burglary.
    - Solution: Encrypting data in transit and at rest, coupled with strict access controls, could have prevented the breach.
- **Adversarial Attacks on AI Models**
    - Problem: Hackers manipulated inputs to an AI image recognition system, causing it to misclassify road signs in self-driving cars.
    - Impact: Such attacks can lead to accidents or system failures, endangering lives.
    - Solution: Use adversarial training and robust defenses to enhance the AI's ability to detect and counteract such manipulations.
- **Surveillance Concerns**
    - Problem: AI systems in public surveillance were used to track individuals without consent, sparking concerns about privacy violations.
    - Impact: This eroded public trust and called for stricter AI regulations.
    - Solution: Develop clear policies on the ethical use of surveillance AI, ensuring transparency and consent mechanisms.

How to Embed Privacy & Security in AI

- **Data Anonymization**
    - Remove personally identifiable information (PII) from datasets used to train AI models.
    - Example: In healthcare, anonymized patient data ensures privacy while enabling valuable research insights.
- **Secure Data Storage and Transfer**
    - Encrypt data at all stages—during collection, storage, and transmission.

    - Example: Banking apps use end-to-end encryption to protect transaction data from being intercepted.
- **Implement Differential Privacy**
    - Add noise to datasets to obscure individual records while preserving aggregate patterns.
    - Example: Apple uses differential privacy in iOS to collect usage statistics without compromising individual user data.
- **Regular Security Audits**
    - Conduct periodic assessments to identify and address vulnerabilities in AI systems.
    - Example: Organizations running facial recognition software must ensure it cannot be spoofed using photos or deepfake videos.
- **User Control and Consent**
    - Allow users to opt-in for data collection and provide clear options to delete or withdraw their data.
    - Example: Social media platforms provide users with tools to download and delete their data, giving them greater control over privacy.

Incorporating privacy and security into AI systems is not just an ethical obligation but a strategic necessity. Organizations prioritizing these principles safeguard user trust, comply with regulations, and future-proof their AI applications against threats. The goal is to create systems that respect individual rights while delivering powerful, transformative benefits.

Inclusiveness

Inclusiveness in AI ensures that systems are designed to accommodate and benefit people from diverse backgrounds, including individuals of varying abilities, socioeconomic statuses, genders, races, languages, and cultures. Inclusive AI actively avoids marginalizing or excluding any demographic group, aiming to serve a global and diverse user base equitably.

Why Inclusiveness Matters

- **Global Accessibility**:AI systems are increasingly deployed worldwide, and failing to account for diversity can alienate or exclude entire communities.
    - Example: Voice recognition systems that primarily understand Western accents may fail to effectively serve non-native English speakers, limiting global usability.
- **Empowering Marginalized Groups**: Inclusiveness in AI can bridge societal gaps by offering solutions tailored to underserved communities.
    - Example: AI-powered education tools designed for rural areas can adapt to local languages and resource constraints, democratizing access to learning.

- **Avoiding Harmful Bias**: Excluding diverse perspectives during development can lead to systems that reinforce stereotypes or perpetuate inequities.
    - Example: Facial recognition software often struggles with accuracy for darker skin tones, leading to disproportionate identification errors.
- **Maximizing Adoption and Usability**: A more inclusive AI system will likely gain widespread acceptance, ensuring it delivers value to a broader audience.
    - Example: An AI chatbot that supports multiple languages can cater to a global audience, improving accessibility and engagement.

Examples of Inclusiveness Challenges in AI

- **Language Barriers**:
    - Problem: AI virtual assistants, like Siri or Alexa, initially supported limited languages and accents, alienating non-English speakers or those with strong regional accents.
    - Impact: This limited the adoption of such technologies outside English-speaking populations.
    - Solution: Expand training datasets to include diverse languages, dialects, and accents to enhance accessibility.
- **Accessibility for People with Disabilities**:
    - Problem: AI-driven websites or applications are often not designed with screen readers or voice commands, making them inaccessible for visually impaired users.
    - Impact: This excludes millions of potential users from accessing digital services.
    - Solution: Integrate accessibility standards like WCAG (Web Content Accessibility Guidelines) and develop inclusive design practices.
- **Cultural Sensitivity**:
    - Problem: AI systems trained on culturally specific datasets might make insensitive or irrelevant recommendations in other regions.
    - Example: A recommendation engine suggesting pork recipes in predominantly Muslim countries could be seen as culturally inappropriate.
    - Solution: Develop culturally aware models by collaborating with local experts and incorporating regional datasets.

How to Embed Inclusiveness in AI

- **Diverse Datasets**:
    - Ensure training datasets represent different demographics, languages, and contexts.
    - Example: A sentiment analysis AI should include text samples from various cultures to capture unique expressions and idioms.
- **Inclusive Design Practices**:

    - Engage diverse user groups during the design and testing phases to ensure AI solutions meet their needs.
    - Example: Microsoft's Seeing AI app for visually impaired users was developed with input from blind and low-vision individuals, ensuring it effectively addressed their challenges.
- **Accessibility Standards**:
    - Incorporate industry standards for accessibility in all AI applications.
    - Example: AI-powered virtual classrooms should support captions for deaf students and voice input for those with mobility challenges.
- **Localization**:
    - Adapt AI systems to local languages, currencies, time zones, and cultural norms to increase relevance and usability.
    - Example: Google Translate continues to add languages and dialects, expanding inclusivity for underrepresented communities.
- **Empowerment Through AI**:
    - Develop tools that address challenges faced by marginalized groups.
    - Example: AI-powered apps for farmers in developing countries can provide localized weather forecasts, pest control advice, and market trends in native languages.

Building inclusive AI systems requires deliberate effort and collaboration with diverse communities. By embracing inclusiveness, organizations can ensure their AI systems are genuinely universal, equitable, and capable of addressing the needs of a varied and global audience.

Transparency

Transparency in AI refers to the clarity and openness with which AI systems are designed, trained, and deployed. This principle ensures that stakeholders, including users, developers, and regulators, can understand how AI systems make decisions, what data they use, and the reasoning behind their outputs. Transparency builds trust by deeming complex AI processes and holding systems accountable.

Why Transparency Matters

- **Trust and Confidence**:

- Users are more likely to trust AI systems when they understand how and why decisions are made.
    - Example: A bank's loan approval AI that explains its decision-making process—such as the factors considered (credit score, income, etc.)can help customers trust the system's Fairness.

- **Accountability and Governance**:
- Transparency enables oversight, ensuring AI systems adhere to ethical and legal standards.
    - Example: If an AI system discriminates in hiring, transparency allows organizations to pinpoint and correct the biases in its algorithm.
- **Reducing the Black Box Effect**: Complex AI systems often function like "black boxes" with opaque internal workings. Transparency helps break this barrier by making processes interpretable.
    - Example: In healthcare, doctors must understand how an AI diagnostic tool arrived at its recommendation to confidently incorporate it into patient care.
- **Regulatory Compliance**: Transparency is critical for meeting legal and regulatory requirements, such as GDPR's mandate to provide explanations for automated decisions.
    - Example: An e-commerce platform using AI for personalized pricing must explain how price differences are determined to comply with regulations.

Examples of Transparency Challenges in AI

- **Opaque Decision-Making**:
    - Problem: An AI-powered hiring tool rejects candidates but does not explain why.
    - Impact: Candidates feel the system is unfair, and the company faces reputational damage.
    - Solution: Provide interpretable feedback, specifying which qualifications or experiences are lacking.
- **Proprietary Algorithms**:
    - Problem: Companies often keep their AI models proprietary, limiting external scrutiny.
    - Impact: Stakeholders cannot assess whether the system is biased or ethical.
    - Solution: Implement explainable AI (XAI) techniques to provide insights without exposing sensitive intellectual property.
- **Complex Models**:
    - Problem: Deep learning models with millions of parameters are inherently difficult to interpret.
    - Impact: Even developers struggle to explain how specific outputs are generated.
    - Solution: Use visualization tools and surrogate models to make these systems more interpretable.

How to Embed Transparency in AI

- **Explainable AI (XAI)**:
  - Design systems that provide clear explanations for their decisions and actions.
  - Example: In a credit scoring AI, explain why an applicant was approved or denied a loan by breaking down contributing factors like payment history and credit utilization.
- **Data Lineage**:
  - Track the origin and processing of data used in training AI systems.
  - Example: An AI that forecasts crop yields should disclose where its data (e.g., weather reports, soil quality) comes from and how it is processed.
- **User Education**:
  - Provide users with accessible information about how the AI system works and its limitations.
  - Example: A recommendation engine on a streaming platform might explain that suggestions are based on viewing history and ratings.
- **Transparent Reporting**:
  - Publish detailed documentation about the system's design, purpose, and potential risks.
  - Example: A government using AI for public services could release a whitepaper outlining how decisions are made and measures taken to ensure Fairness.
- **Third-Party Audits**:
  - Allow independent organizations to review and verify the system's Fairness and functionality.
  - Example: AI models in credit scoring can be audited to ensure they do not discriminate against specific demographic groups.

Organizations can bridge the gap between technological complexity and user understanding by embedding transparency into AI systems. This openness fosters trust, ensures ethical compliance, and equips all stakeholders to engage with AI responsibly and confidently.

Accountability

Accountability in AI refers to the obligation of individuals, organizations, and systems to take responsibility for the actions and outcomes produced by AI technologies. It ensures that AI systems operate ethically sound, legally compliant, and align with societal values. Accountability provides a mechanism for holding developers, organizations, and users responsible for the consequences of AI decisions.

Why Accountability Matters

- **Ethical Responsibility**: AI systems have significant power over decisions that affect people's lives. Accountability ensures these systems are used ethically and responsibly.
    - Example: In autonomous vehicles, accountability mechanisms ensure that if an accident occurs, the manufacturer, developers, or responsible parties can be liable for any negligence or failure in system design.
- **Trust and Credibility**: When organizations are held accountable for AI actions, trust builds with users, stakeholders, and the public.
    - Example: A company that uses AI for automated customer support should be accountable for ensuring its system does not provide misleading or harmful advice.
- **Preventing Harm**: Clear accountability prevents AI systems from being used in ways that can cause harm to individuals or communities.
    - Example: AI systems used in criminal justice should be accountable for ensuring they do not perpetuate biases or wrongly influence sentencing or parole decisions.
- **Legal and Regulatory Compliance**: Accountability ensures AI systems comply with data privacy laws or consumer protection regulations.
    - Example: A retail company using AI to price products dynamically must be accountable for ensuring its algorithms do not violate anti-price gouging laws.

Examples of Accountability Challenges in AI

- **Unclear Ownership**:
    - Problem: It is difficult to pinpoint who is responsible when an AI system causes harm.
    - Impact: Individuals affected by harmful AI decisions may lack recourse without clear accountability.
    - Solution: Organizations must define clear accountability structures, assigning responsibility to developers, users, and companies involved in AI design and deployment.
- **Lack of Auditing Mechanisms**:
    - Problem: Some AI systems are not regularly audited or reviewed for their performance and ethical implications.
    - Impact: AI systems may continue to operate with unchecked biases or flaws, leading to unfair or unsafe outcomes.
    - Solution: Implement regular third-party audits to evaluate AI systems, ensuring they meet ethical standards and perform as intended.
- **Opaque Decision-Making Processes**:
    - Problem: When an AI makes a decision, it may be unclear who should be held accountable, especially if its reasoning is not transparent.

  - Impact: This can lead to unaddressed errors, harm, or unethical decisions with no clear parties responsible.
  - Solution: Develop AI systems with transparent, interpretable decision-making processes and documentation that can help pinpoint where and why a decision was made.

How to Embed Accountability in AI

- **Clear Accountability Frameworks**:
  - Establish a clear structure defining who is responsible for each AI development, deployment, and operation aspect.
  - Example: In healthcare AI, medical professionals, software developers, and regulatory bodies should share responsibility to ensure the AI's proper use.
- **Regular Audits and Monitoring**:
  - Conduct independent audits to evaluate AI systems' Fairness, safety, and effectiveness. Regular monitoring can identify potential issues before they become serious problems.
  - Example: AI tools used in recruitment could undergo periodic audits to detect biases or unequal treatment of candidates based on demographic factors.
- **Establishing Legal and Ethical Guidelines**:
  - Develop clear legal and ethical guidelines that define responsible AI behavior. Ensure these guidelines are followed throughout the system's lifecycle.
  - Example: A finance company that uses AI for trading should have guidelines to prevent market manipulation or unfair advantages for specific groups.
- **Human-in-the-Loop Systems**:
  - Implement systems where human oversight is built into decision-making, ensuring a person can always be held accountable for final decisions.
  - Example: In healthcare, AI can assist doctors in diagnosing conditions, but the doctor remains accountable for confirming the diagnosis and treatment plan.
- **Transparency in Reporting Mistakes and Outcomes**:
  - Ensure that AI systems are equipped with mechanisms to report mistakes and take corrective actions when they go wrong.
  - Example: If an AI recommendation system suggests a harmful product to users, it should provide a clear path for reporting the mistake, and the company should take responsibility for rectifying the issue.

By embedding accountability into AI systems, organizations can ensure that AI technologies are used responsibly and moderately. This responsibility is key to maintaining public trust, preventing harm, and ensuring that AI systems benefit everyone equitably and transparently.

Legal and Ethical Aspects

The conversation about AI ethics is not new. With the rapid rise of generative AI models—capable of creating text, images, music, and even deepfakes—the stakes have never been higher. These systems can generate content at an unprecedented scale, making it crucial to ensure that they operate within the law, align with ethical principles, and foster public trust.

Let us explore why legal and ethical aspects are the cornerstones of responsible AI development.

Regulatory Compliance: Navigating the Legal Landscape

AI must operate within the boundaries of existing laws, which vary across jurisdictions and continue to evolve. Companies deploying AI-powered solutions must ensure compliance with data protection laws, intellectual property rights, consumer protection regulations, and anti-discrimination policies. Failure to comply can result in legal penalties, financial losses, and reputational damage.

Example: The General Data Protection Regulation (GDPR) in the European Union requires AI systems that process personal data to adhere to strict privacy and security measures. If a chatbot trained on customer interactions stores sensitive data without user consent, it could result in severe legal consequences, including fines of up to 4% of a company's global revenue.

Since laws differ across countries, organizations developing AI solutions for global markets must adapt their AI models to comply with regional regulations, which is complex and critical for responsible AI governance.

Ethical Responsibility: Ensuring Fairness, Transparency, and Accountability

Even if an AI system complies with laws, it does not necessarily mean it is ethical. Ethics goes beyond legal constraints, addressing moral concerns such as:

- Fairness: Does the AI model treat all individuals equitably, regardless of race, gender, or socioeconomic status?
- Transparency: Can humans understand the AI's decision-making process?
- Accountability: Who is responsible when AI causes harm?

Example: AI-driven facial recognition systems have been found to misidentify people of color at higher rates than white individuals, leading to wrongful arrests and discrimination. While some AI developers claim their models are "impartial," ethical AI practices demand continuous bias testing, fairness audits, and accountability mechanisms to prevent discriminatory outcomes.

Organizations must establish clear ethical guidelines and implement bias detection frameworks to ensure AI decisions align with societal values.

Public Trust: A Prerequisite for AI Adoption

AI adoption depends heavily on public trust. If users believe AI systems are unfair, deceptive, or intrusive, they will resist their implementation, ultimately limiting AI's potential benefits.

Building trust requires:

- Transparency - Clearly explaining how AI makes decisions.
- User Consent - Allowing users to opt in or out of AI-driven processes.
- Ethical AI Development - Ensuring AI is developed with societal well-being in mind.

Example: In the healthcare industry, AI-powered diagnostic tools are gaining traction, but many patients and doctors hesitate to rely on them. By providing explainability mechanisms (e.g., showing why an AI model predicted a particular disease based on medical images), AI developers can improve trust and increase acceptance of AI in critical domains like healthcare.

Preventing AI Misuse: Averting Unintended Harm

AI can be weaponized for malicious purposes through deepfake technology, misinformation campaigns, biased hiring algorithms, or cyberattacks. Preventing misuse requires proactive governance, strong ethical guidelines, and legal frameworks that anticipate potential risks before they become actual threats.

Example: In recent years, deepfake videos have been used to impersonate politicians, spread false information, and even commit financial fraud. Without strict AI content labeling and detection mechanisms, AI-generated misinformation could erode democracy and public trust in the media.

Accountability: Who is Responsible When AI Goes Wrong?

One of the biggest unanswered questions in AI ethics is who is accountable when AI makes a mistake. If an autonomous car crashes, who is legally liable—the manufacturer, the software developer, or the owner? AI must have clear accountability structures that define responsibility for errors, ensuring that individuals have legal recourse if AI decisions harm them.

Example: In a landmark case in 2023, a self-driving car hit a pedestrian due to a sensor failure. The manufacturer argued that the AI system was not fully autonomous and required human oversight, while the user claimed they relied entirely on AI decision-making. This case underscores the urgent need for legal clarity in AI accountability.

How to Embed Legal and Ethical Aspects in AI Development

To ensure AI is developed and deployed responsibly, organizations should adopt the following best practices:

Conduct Regular AI Compliance Audits

- Review AI models periodically to ensure they comply with data protection, anti-discrimination, and intellectual property laws.
- Implement internal audit teams to assess compliance with regulatory frameworks like GDPR, the AI Act, and U.S. AI regulations.

Implement Ethical AI Guidelines and Training

- Train AI developers, data scientists, and business leaders on AI ethics, bias mitigation, and responsible AI design.
- Establish company-wide AI ethics policies, ensuring every AI system aligns with moral principles.

Engage Diverse Stakeholders in AI Development

- Collaborate with ethicists, legal experts, civil rights organizations, and affected communities to ensure AI models reflect diverse perspectives.
- Prioritize inclusive AI development to mitigate biases that disproportionately harm marginalized groups.

Ensure AI Transparency and Explainability

- Develop AI models with explainable AI (XAI) techniques so users understand why an AI system decided.
- Publish AI transparency reports detailing how AI models are trained, validated, and monitored for ethical compliance.

Establish AI Redress Mechanisms for Harmed Individuals

- Provide legal safeguards ensuring that individuals can challenge unfair AI decisions.
- Implement processes for AI-driven outcomes, such as job rejections or financial loan denials.

Legal and ethical considerations in AI are not optional—they are essential for ensuring AI remains a force for good. Companies that proactively embed legal safeguards, uphold ethical standards, and prioritize transparency will not only avoid regulatory penalties but also earn public trust, foster innovation, and create AI systems that truly benefit humanity.

As we continue pushing the boundaries of generative AI, the question is no longer "Can AI do this?" but "Should AI do this?"

Conclusion

These principles do not exist in isolation—they work together to form a holistic framework for Responsible AI:

- Fairness ensures inclusivity.
- Privacy and security bolster transparency and trust.
- Accountability drives reliability and safety.

Adhering to these principles can make AI a tool that enhances productivity and aligns with ethical and societal values. Let me know if you would like further elaboration or if we should move on to the next section. Responsible AI is not a technical afterthought but a cornerstone for building trust, Fairness, and sustainability in an AI-driven world. By addressing bias, accountability, privacy, and transparency issues, Responsible AI ensures that technology works for everyone—not just a privileged few. With Responsible AI, the promise of AI can be realized—empowering innovation without compromising the values that bind us as a society.

Exercise: Test Your Understanding

Answer the following questions and test your understanding of learning from

Chapter 11:

Q. 1. What is Responsible AI, and why is it important?

Q. 2. How can AI systems amplify existing biases, and what are the consequences?

Q. 3. What are the core principles of Responsible AI, and how do they contribute to ethical AI development?

Q. 4. Why is transparency important in AI, and what are some associated challenges?

Q. 5. How can organizations ensure AI systems are legally and ethically compliant?

Appendix-A

Answers - Test your understanding

CHAPTER 1

Answers to test your understanding, `Chapter 1`

`Ans.1.` Generative AI can enhance creativity by providing tools that assist and inspire artists, musicians, and writers. For example, AI models like StyleGAN can generate unique visual art pieces, while MuseNet can compose music in various styles. In writing, models like GPT-3 can help authors generate story ideas, draft content, or offer alternative phrasings. These tools expand creative possibilities and enable new forms of artistic expression.

`Ans.2.` Transformer architectures revolutionized NLP by enabling parallel processing of entire data sequences through the self-attention mechanism, which allows for better handling of long-range dependencies. Real-world applications include machine translation, text summarization, sentiment analysis, and conversational AI models like ChatGPT.

`Ans.3.` GANs consist of two neural networks: the generator, which creates data, and the discriminator, which evaluates its authenticity. They work in tandem to improve the quality of the data generated. An example application is medical imaging, where GANs can generate synthetic MRI or CT scans to augment training datasets for diagnostic tools.

`Ans.4.` The self-attention mechanism in transformer networks allows the model to evaluate the importance of different parts of a data sequence simultaneously rather than sequentially, as in RNNs and LSTMs. This enables transformers to handle long-range dependencies more effectively, making them particularly powerful for tasks like text generation and translation where context is crucial.

`Ans.5.` Generative AI can enhance creativity by providing tools that assist and inspire artists, musicians, and writers. For example, AI models like StyleGAN can generate unique visual art pieces, while MuseNet can compose music in various styles. In writing, models like GPT-3 can help authors generate story ideas, draft content, or offer alternative phrasings. These tools expand creative possibilities and enable new forms of artistic expression.

CHAPTER 2

Answers to test your understanding, `Chapter 2`

`Ans.1.` Organizations can leverage the complementary strengths of LLMs and SLMs by strategically deploying each model based on the specific requirements of their tasks. LLMs can be used for complex, high-value tasks that require deep contextual understanding, such as strategic decision-making, trend analysis, and creative content generation. On the other hand, SLMs can handle routine, domain-specific tasks that require speed and efficiency, such as real-time customer support, data entry, and simple diagnostics. Adopting a hybrid approach can help organizations optimize operations, reduce costs, and improve overall productivity. Additionally, continuous monitoring and fine-tuning of these models can help organizations stay ahead of industry trends, adapt to new challenges, and maintain a competitive edge. This balanced use of LLMs and SLMs encourages innovation by enabling more dynamic and responsive business strategies.

`Ans.2.` Integrating LLMs and SLMs could significantly democratize access to high-quality language processing tools in these industries. Traditionally, only larger firms with substantial resources can afford the computational power and data necessary to leverage LLMs for tasks like contract review or medical diagnostics. Smaller firms or institutions can harness advanced AI capabilities by combining LLMs for complex, nuanced tasks and SLMs for more routine, specific functions. This hybrid approach allows for more cost-effective and efficient operations, potentially leveling the playing field and encouraging innovation and competition in these critical sectors.

`Ans.3.` SLMs (Small Language Models) are designed for highly specialized tasks with lower computational demands, making them ideal for real-time applications, edge devices, and cost-efficient deployments. On the other hand, LLMs (Large Language Models) excel in complex reasoning, deep contextual understanding, and large-scale applications but require significant computing resources and cost.

`Ans.4.` SLMs face three main challenges that can impact their effectiveness. Limited generalization is a key issue, as these models struggle to adapt beyond their narrow training scope. Additionally, SLMs are highly dependent on high-quality, domain-specific data, which can be costly and scarce. Lastly, overfitting risks arise when training on small datasets, leading to poor performance on unseen scenarios.

`Ans.5.` Small Language Models (SLMs) help reduce AI adoption costs by offering several advantages. They require less computational power, making them suitable for deployment on on-premises servers or edge devices. Their ability to be fine-tuned quickly with smaller, domain-specific datasets also reduces time and cost. Additionally, SLMs deliver faster real-time insights, which are particularly valuable for use cases like retail price adjustments or optimizing factory production lines. This combination of efficiency and cost-effectiveness makes SLMs appealing for businesses looking to leverage AI without significant infrastructure investment.

CHAPTER 3

Answers to test your understanding, `Chapter 3`

`Ans.1.` Vector databases challenge traditional data storage by moving from the rigid, row-and-column format to a more flexible high-dimensional vector representation. This shift allows for a nuanced understanding of data relationships, enabling applications like semantic search and personalized recommendations.

`Ans.2.` The dot product measures the product of the magnitudes of two vectors and the cosine of the angle between them, considering both magnitude and direction. This makes it particularly useful in applications where both factors are meaningful, such as stock price movement analysis. Cosine similarity, on the other hand, focuses solely on the angle between two vectors, disregarding their magnitudes. This measure is ideal for comparing the relative orientation of high-dimensional data points and is commonly used in natural language processing and recommendation systems. Euclidean distance calculates the straight-line distance between two vectors in a multidimensional space, making it useful in applications where the absolute positioning of vectors is important, such as in image recognition and anomaly detection. Each measure provides a different perspective on the relationships between vectors, allowing for versatile applications in vector databases.

`Ans.3.` Vector embeddings are numerical representations of data points in a multidimensional space designed to capture relationships, meanings, and contextual similarities. They are fundamental to the functionality of vector databases as they allow for the storage and retrieval of high-dimensional vectors while preserving the semantic meaning and relationships between data points.

`Ans.4.` Vector databases find practical applications in advanced search and semantic relationships, recommendation systems, and generative AI. In advanced search, vector databases enable semantic searches by understanding the meaning behind data points rather than relying on exact matches, which can recommend items similar in style or color in an e-commerce platform. They deliver highly personalized suggestions for recommendation systems by analyzing vectors representing user preferences and product attributes.

`Ans.5.` Different vector indexing techniques contribute to the efficiency of vector databases by optimizing the way high-dimensional data is organized and retrieved. KD-Trees partition the data space into hyper-rectangular regions, making them practical for low-dimensional data but less for high-dimensional datasets. Ball Trees use hyperspheres for partitioning, better suited for datasets with irregular distributions. Locality-sensitive hashing (LSH) reduces the dimensionality of vectors while preserving relative distances, enabling faster searches. Hierarchical Navigable Small World (HNSW) graphs create a network of nodes and edges, allowing for fast approximate nearest neighbor searches. Each technique offers unique advantages, making vector databases versatile and efficient in handling complex data retrieval tasks.

CHAPTER 4

Answers to test your understanding, **`Chapter 4`**

`Ans.1.` RAG enhances AI by integrating relevant, up-to-date information from external sources into the generation process, ensuring more accurate and contextually relevant responses.

`Ans.2.` The three key components are the Retriever (fetches relevant data), the Augmenter (organizes and refines data), and the Generator (produces the final, coherent response).

`Ans.3.` Vector RAG uses vector databases to find semantically similar data points, while Graph RAG uses knowledge graphs to understand and retrieve information based on relationships between data entities. Graph RAG is helpful for complex queries involving relationships between entities, such as risk assessment, vendor tracking, and compliance mapping, where understanding the context and connections between data points is crucial.

`Ans.4.` The Generator uses the augmented data and user query to produce a coherent, contextually accurate response, leveraging its deep language understanding to provide a natural and insightful answer.

`Ans.5.` The Augmentation Engine manages token limits by selecting the most relevant information from the retrieved data, ensuring that the language model processes a manageable and pertinent subset within its context window.

CHAPTER 5

Answers to test your understanding, `Chapter 5`

`Ans.1.` RAG excels in retrieving accurate, context-rich information from external sources, but it falters with complex, domain-specific queries that require deep understanding, such as legal analysis or personalized healthcare recommendations.

`Ans.2.` Fine-tuning customizes pre-trained models with domain-specific knowledge, enhancing precision and relevance, which allows AI to handle specialized tasks effectively where RAG alone may not suffice.

`Ans.3.` Fine-tuning requires high-quality, annotated training data, significant computational resources, and expertise. Additionally, there must be a balance between maintaining generality and achieving deep specialization.

`Ans.4.` A hybrid approach leverages the strengths of both methods, using RAG for versatile information retrieval and fine-tuning for specialized, context-aware responses, making AI models adaptable and deeply knowledgeable.

`Ans.5.` Fine-tuning can perpetuate or amplify biases present in training data. Integrating safeguards ensures the model's outputs are fair, ethical, and representative of diverse perspectives, maintaining trust and reliability in AI applications.

CHAPTER 6

Answers to test your understanding, `Chapter 6`

`Ans.1.` A prompt is an input provided to a Generative AI model to guide its response. It is important because well-crafted prompts ensure that the AI produces relevant, precise, and contextually appropriate outputs, enhancing the effectiveness and efficiency of AI interactions.

`Ans.2.` Best practices include being specific, using examples to clarify intent, setting clear expectations, incorporating constraints like word limits or tone, and leveraging role-specific perspectives to align the output with the target audience's needs.

`Ans.3.` Zero-shot prompting relies on the AI's pre-trained knowledge without providing prior examples, which is suitable for simple queries. Few-shot prompting provides the

AI with examples to guide its response, which is helpful for tasks requiring nuanced or contextual understanding.

Ans.4. Iterative refinement is crucial because it allows for continuous improvement of prompts based on AI's output. Users can enhance AI responses' precision, relevance, and quality by analyzing and adjusting prompts.

Ans.5. Chain-of-thought prompting improves AI responses by guiding the model through a structured, step-by-step reasoning process. This ensures logical clarity and accuracy, particularly for tasks requiring multi-step reasoning, resulting in more coherent and reliable outputs.

CHAPTER 7

Answers to test your understanding, **Chapter 7**

Ans.1. The primary considerations include the project goals and scope, compatibility with existing systems, ease of use and learning curve, and community support and documentation.

Ans.2. LangChain simplifies development by providing an ecosystem of tools, integrations, and abstractions, such as chat models, prompt engineering, memory management, and seamless integration with external systems, which streamline the entire lifecycle of LLM-based applications.

Ans.3. The Kernel in Semantic Kernel acts as a Dependency Injection (DI) container that manages services and plugins essential for running AI-driven applications, enabling seamless interaction between AI models and application functionalities.

Ans.4. The key benefits include efficient workflows, reusable components, built-in memory management, seamless integration with external systems, scalability, reduced complexity, and fostering collaboration, allowing developers to focus on innovation and solving real-world problems.

Ans.5. Prompt engineering is crucial for effectively directing AI models to perform specific tasks. LangChain manages it through predefined prompt templates, few-shot prompting techniques, and example selectors, which standardize and dynamically adapt prompts to improve model performance and reusability.

CHAPTER 8

Answers to test your understanding, `Chapter 8`

`Ans.1.` The main challenges in multi-agent conversations within Multi-Agent Systems include coordination complexity, conflict resolution, and scalability. Coordination complexity arises from managing transitions and ensuring coherence in interactions among multiple agents. Conflict resolution involves designing mechanisms to address competing goals and resource allocation fairly. Scalability challenges pertain to maintaining system performance as the number of agents and interactions grows. However, these challenges also present opportunities. Effective coordination and structured conversation patterns can significantly reduce time and effort for complex tasks, enhancing overall system efficiency. Flexible conversation patterns, such as dynamic and nested interactions, allow agents to adapt to changing conditions, providing resilience and robustness. Additionally, enabling multi-agent interactions facilitates collaborative problem-solving, leveraging diverse expertise to tackle more complex and dynamic issues.

`Ans.2.` Multi-agent systems (MAS) offer significant advantages over single-agent systems, particularly in handling complex, dynamic environments. The primary benefits include scalability, resilience, and adaptability. MAS enables multiple agents to collaborate, negotiate, and pool their expertise to solve intricate and interconnected problems, which single-agent systems find challenging. This collaboration allows MAS to adapt to rapidly changing conditions and manage multi-faceted tasks more effectively. Additionally, MAS can scale quickly by adding more agents to handle new tasks or domains without disrupting the entire system, making them more suitable for real-world applications where conditions and requirements constantly evolve.

`Ans.3.` The core characteristics of Multi-Agent Systems (MAS) include autonomy, local views, decentralized control, adaptability, and interaction. Autonomy means that each Agent operates independently, making decisions and taking actions based on its internal processes without direct external control. Local views refer to each Agent having limited information about the overall system or the state of other agents, promoting scalability by focusing on localized tasks. Decentralized control indicates no central controller; control is distributed among agents, enhancing the system's scalability and robustness. Adaptability allows agents to adjust their behavior in response to changes in their environment, goals, or the actions of other agents. Lastly, interaction involves agents communicating and interacting through cooperation, competition, and negotiation to achieve common or competing goals, which is crucial for achieving global system objectives and resolving conflicts.

`Ans.4.` The three main conversation patterns in Multi-Agent Systems are direct two-agent conversations, coordinated multi-agent conversations, and conversations with varying levels of autonomy. Direct two-agent conversations are the simplest form, where two autonomous agents communicate directly to achieve a specific goal or exchange information. Coordinated multi-agent conversations involve complex interactions among multiple agents, which can be hierarchical, dynamic, or nested. Hierarchical conversations have a lead agent managing inputs from subordinate agents, dynamic group conversations allow multiple agents to interact fluidly with a conversation manager overseeing the process, and nested conversations break down complex tasks into sub-conversations for detailed problem-solving. Conversations with varying levels of autonomy balance agent independence with human oversight, ranging from entirely autonomous interactions where agents make decisions independently to human-guided conversations where agents assist by providing insights or automating subtasks.

`Ans.5.` Modularity and scalability are crucial design principles for developing robust multi-Agent AI systems. Modularity involves designing each Agent as an independent, cooperative unit, akin to a LEGO brick, allowing seamless integration, updating, testing, or replacement without impacting the overall system. This modular approach simplifies maintenance and enhances system flexibility.

CHAPTER 9

Answers to test your understanding, `Chapter 9`

`Ans.1.` The primary business functions discussed are Procurement, HR, Legal, and Finance.

`Ans.2.` Generative AI enhances the Procurement process by automating repetitive, low-value tasks, allowing procurement teams to focus on strategic initiatives like supplier innovation, risk mitigation, and sustainability. It uses a multi-agent system to manage category mapping, policy compliance, spend insight, supplier evaluation, and negotiation.

`Ans.3.` Generative AI improves the talent acquisition process by automating the creation of tailored job descriptions, intelligent resume screening, personalized candidate outreach, and analyzing interview transcripts to identify key traits and fit, thus streamlining and personalizing the hiring process.

Ans.4. Key benefits include automated clause detection, real-time redlining suggestions, compliance checks, and risk mitigation. This reduces manual effort, ensures consistency, and enhances accuracy in contract management.

Ans.5. Generative AI can automatically generate detailed financial narratives, summarize key financial metrics, and translate them into actionable insights.

CHAPTER 10

Answers to test your understanding, **Chapter 10**

Ans.1. Generative AI transforms Manufacturing by optimizing production processes, enhancing product design and prototyping, improving predictive maintenance, and streamlining supply chains through intelligent automation and data analysis.

Ans.2. In the automobile and mobility sectors, Generative AI is used to develop advanced in-vehicle assistants, enhance personalized customer experiences, support smart dealership operations, and aid in the design and development of autonomous driving technologies and electric vehicles.

Ans.3. In financial services, Generative AI improves fraud detection, risk management, and customer personalization. It enhances operational efficiency through AI-driven contact center transformation, advanced knowledge search capabilities, and automated pitch book generation.

Ans.4. Generative AI accelerates product design and prototyping innovation by generating multiple design options based on predefined parameters, enabling teams to evaluate and select the best designs backed by data and simulated performance tests.

Ans.5. Generative AI enhances customer experience personalization in the automotive industry by analyzing customer data to provide tailored marketing offers, real-time AI-driven support, and ownership insights. It can enable personalized interactions and recommendations based on individual driving habits and preferences.

CHAPTER 11

Answers to test your understanding, **Chapter 11**

Ans.1. Responsible AI embeds Fairness, accountability, and transparency principles into every stage of AI development and deployment. It is crucial because it ensures AI systems are designed to be technically robust, socially, and ethically sound, thereby preventing the amplification of biases, privacy violations, misinformation, lack of accountability, and erosion of trust in technology.

Ans.2. AI systems learn from data, and if that data contains societal, historical, or systemic biases, the AI will reflect and amplify them. Consequences include perpetuating gender inequality in hiring practices, misidentifying people with darker skin tones in facial recognition, and reinforcing over-policing in specific neighborhoods

Ans.3. The core principles include Fairness, Reliability and safety, Privacy and security, Inclusiveness, Transparency, and Accountability. These principles ensure AI technologies are developed and deployed ethically, treating all users equitably, performing consistently and safely, protecting user data, accommodating diverse needs, being understandable, and holding developers and organizations accountable.

Ans.4. Transparency builds trust by making AI processes understandable and accountable. It is important because it enables oversight, ensures adherence to ethical and legal standards, and reduces the "black box" effect. Challenges include opaque decision-making, proprietary algorithms, and the complexity of deep learning models.

Ans.5. Organizations should conduct regular AI compliance audits, implement ethical AI guidelines and training, engage diverse stakeholders in AI development, ensure AI transparency and explainability, and establish AI redress mechanisms for harmed individuals. These measures help align AI systems with regulatory requirements and ethical standards, fostering public trust and preventing misuse.

JOIN US ON THE ARCCHIE PUBLICATIONS DISCORD SERVER

Connect with fellow readers, authors, and enthusiasts to discuss all things related to our publications and the exciting world of AI, programming, and learning. Share your insights, ask questions, and engage in vibrant discussions to expand your knowledge and inspire creativity. Take advantage of this opportunity to be part of a dynamic community dedicated to exploring the frontiers of technology and innovation. Join our Discord Server today and be part of the ARCCHIE Publications community!

https://discord.gg/z26SenmpEt